Spiritual Enlightenment

The Intelligent Way to Awaken, Enlighten, Discover Your True Self, and Find Liberation

SMITHA JAGADISH

Spiritual Enlightenment: The Intelligent Way to
Awaken, Enlighten, Discover Your True Self, and find
Liberation © Copyright 2020 Smitha Jagadish

Although the author and publisher have made every effort to ensure that the information in this book was correct at press time, the author and publisher do not assume and hereby disclaim any liability to any party for any loss, damage, or disruption caused by errors or omissions, whether such errors or omissions result from negligence, accident, or any other cause.

Adherence to all applicable laws and regulations, including international, federal, state, and local governing professional licensing, business practises, advertising, and all other aspects of doing business in the UK, Canada, US or any other jurisdiction, is the sole responsibility of the reader and consumer.

Neither the author nor the publisher assumes any responsibility or liability whatsoever on behalf of the consumer or reader of this material. Any perceived slight of any individual or organization is purely unintentional.

The resources in this book are provided for informational purposes only. They should not be used to replace the specialized training and professional judgment of a health care or mental health care professional.

Neither the author nor the publisher can be held responsible for using the information provided within this book. Please always consult a trained professional before making any decision regarding treatment of yourself or others.

For more information, email: info@theschoolforenlightenment.com

GET YOUR FREE GIFT!

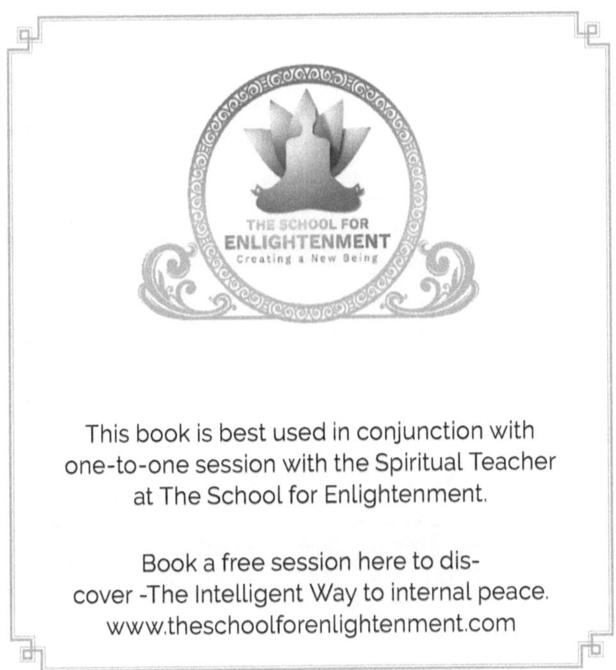

This book is best used in conjunction with
one-to-one session with the Spiritual Teacher
at The School for Enlightenment.

Book a free session here to discover -The Intelligent Way to internal peace.
www.theschoolforenlightenment.com

To get the best experience with this book, readers who
book one-on-one sessions with the spiritual teacher learn
a new way to implement the next steps needed to experience enlightenment and reach internal peace.

You can book a free session by emailing info@
theschoolforenlightenment.com.
Please also visit:
www.theschoolforenlightenment.com

Dedication

This book is dedicated to all the suffering souls wishing to end the suffering and take these necessary steps to enlighten and liberate themselves to live a beautiful life of peace!

LOVE TO YOU ALL!

Contents

Introduction...ix

Part 1: Born into Spirituality... 1
    Chapter 1   Land of Spirituality.................................. 3
    Chapter 2   Growing Up With Values........................ 9
    Chapter 3   Disciplined Life.....................................13
    Chapter 4   Experiencing Emptiness 17
    Chapter 5   Running Away From It All......................21
    Chapter 6   Knowing Nothing...................................25
    Chapter 7   Accumulating Knowledge 29
    Chapter 8   Wanting It All..33
    Chapter 9   Finding a Guide.....................................37
    Chapter 10 The Family Life.....................................41

Part 2: Practises to Enlightenment 47
    Chapter 11 Power Flow Practise 49
    Chapter 12 Empty Through Living Practise 59
    Chapter 13 The Essence of Questioning Practise 65
    Chapter 14 Observing the Truth Practise 71

Part 3: Levels of Being..77

    Chapter 15   Level 1: Awakening.................................79

    Chapter 16   Level 2: Enlightenment...........................85

    Chapter 17   Level 3: True Love 91

    Chapter 18   Level 4: New Consciousness....................95

    Chapter 19   Level 5: Liberation 99

Part 4: Purpose of The School for Enlightenment............. 101

    Chapter 20   Questions and Answers....................... 103

    Chapter 21   The School For Enlightenment............. 113

    Chapter 22   The Programs...................................... 119

Acknowledgements...123

Author Bio 125

Introduction

Do you feel stuck or confused in life? Do you feel lost in this world? Are you tired of searching for who you truly are? Have you found ways to overcome your suffering?

If you have ever asked yourself, "What is my purpose in life?" or wondered what life is all about but never found any answers, then this book will reveal to you a new pathway out of your confusion and suffering. It will show you—The Intelligent Way to find internal peace.

In this book, you'll learn about my early unconscious spiritual life led in India—complete with its confusion and beliefs of every religion and form of spirituality around me. Then you'll learn about my move to England, where I experienced awakening, enlightenment, discovered my true self, and finally became liberated.

You'll learn my perspective about exactly what we are here for in this life. After experiencing three decades of spiritual life in both the East and West, I offer insight into the true meaning of spirituality. Through the personal journey of finding inner peace, I explain the stages of spiritual enlightenment and several effective practises I discovered through my own spiritual journey.

The early years of our conscious experience are essential to realizing who we truly are and our purpose in life. Having gone through a painful and unfruitful search for a spiritual guide, I explain my reasons for opening The School for Enlightenment and its mission and purpose to help everyone discover their true self and be liberated in life. As a spiritual teacher, I now help many on their spiritual journey.

This book is a complete one-stop guide for all spiritual seekers—you need look no further. To find spiritual growth, you only need simple truth and expert guidance.

Clearing false ideas and beliefs and engaging in the right thinking can open the door to reality. This book helps you learn how to recognize your dormant intelligence and will teach you practises to help you unite your new consciousness with life to reach liberation.

Part 1

Born into Spirituality

Chapter 1

Land of Spirituality

I was born into a Hindu family in India, and with religious ceremonies seeming to happen every other day, I did not understand what was going on. Confusion surrounded me growing up, and people did not seem to know what they wanted in life, yet it seemed like they were running after something even if they didn't know what they were doing.

As a young child growing up in this confusion, I desired to know what was going on. What was this confusion about? I received no explanation, and the only choice was to follow others.

Growing up, I realized life lessons were not offered in school, and I had no other place to learn about life—confusion and chaos were all that was offered. If you were lucky enough, your parents might have explored life a little, and you would hope they might lead you in the right direction.

But with a large population in India, life was often occupied with all the daily activities we did to survive, and it was a busy and hectic life. A growing child needs a guide, a direction, and peace around them to discover life. When you see confused people around you, you learn confusion.

As a grown-up, I now realize, having access to something like a *School for Enlightenment* could have helped me seek the truth. Even though a few spiritual schools were available, they were mainly for boys. Somehow women were steered away from spirituality.

While growing up, somebody told me, "You ask God for whatever you want, you will get it, but you must do many prayers and make him happy to get what you want." From this, I learned that praying meant questioning God and asking for things.

Being an active child, I didn't pray to God much. It was time-consuming and difficult. As a child, you need quick results; however, I did my fair share of praying as there was no other choice.

I eventually realised that the path of religion and devotion was difficult for me. Loving God more than oneself was quite a hard thing to do as a child. Every child thinks, "Where is God? I can't see whom I am praying to." Thus, loving a god I could not see was a challenging task.

But eventually, I managed to learn the art of prayer. I remember my mother showed me how to pray to God and how the devotional path works. She was very devoted to gods and goddesses, and she prayed for more than four to five hours each day.

Following my mother's guidance, every day I prayed for an hour and thought of a wish I wanted to experience. I told God, "If you give me this, I will write your name a thousand times, or go to temple the next ten weeks, or fast for two days; or I will put a lovely garland in a particular temple any which way to please you."

Even though I did not understand what Hinduism was, as I was never taught enough about it, I just carried on this process of making a deal with God every single day. He would deliver whatever I asked for, and I continued this deal with God for many years.

India is vastly diverse in its religions, traditions, and cultures. There is so much to learn and know about faith and spirituality that one lifetime is not enough to understand it all. There were so many stories, beliefs, dogmas, superstitions, black magic, theories, and ideas that it is all too confusing for anyone.

For example, as soon as you are born, parents must check your date and time, so they can run to the astrologer to ask, "What will my child become? Is a good or bad life coming his or her way? When will my child be married? Is she or he going to have a great job? When will my child have his or her first child?"

When a child is born, parents immediately take on the burden of that child's future life. They feel that they must live their child's life. The worry for their child begins immediately. They do not know how to let their child live their life and just be supportive parents. If the astrologer says that the child has a great future, then the parents stay happy, whereas if they are told the end was looking grim, they would do hundreds of different ceremonies to change the luck. Such was the scene around me growing up.

A vast majority of people in India believe in one religion or another. The deep commitment people have to religion, and the extreme devotion to faith is unbelievable. It is as though there is a competition as to who can be God's favourite child and who can go to this extra length in experiencing the divine.

I witnessed people go without food for many days to please God. People would spend thousands of rupees decorating God's idol with lavish, grand, and expensive jewellery to please him. Some would sleep on a bed of thorns or walk in the fire to be his favourite child. When I was growing up, these things had a remarkable impact on me.

I used to watch mythological stories about Lord Krishna, Vishnu, Shiva, and Buddha. Every single day my mother would read many books about divine beings to me. Even though spirituality and religion are separate but misunderstood in India, I only noticed spirituality connecting with me rather than any religion. I was interested in discovering myself rather than believing in anything.

Even at a young age, I could see people admired the qualities of gods and goddesses, but they worshipped them for having these powers and qualities. But they never saw how to embody those qualities for themselves. Spirituality was about discovering those god qualities within us and acting on them. Looking back, it seemed as though I was born into spirituality. There was no escape; it was all around me and in me.

Somehow, I immediately connected with spirituality from the age of five. This was the only clearly conscious experience of my growing life—in contrast, every other thing seemed blurred and unconscious.

India is a land of spirituality. I connected with Buddha, Mahavira, Ramana, and many other saints and rishis. The simplicity and peace projected by these people attracted me to such a great degree that I could see nothing else. I was deeply moved by their depth of human compassion and love. It was as though I could see their pain of humanity. I could see they knew the answers to human suffering, and they wanted to help.

Spirituality, in my eyes, was about experiencing the divine within yourself. It was about going deep within you to see who you really are. It was about exploring life, experimenting with it, and discovering the truth for yourself rather than following the truth of others or books. I was fascinated by deeply exploring broad interests—learning everything from scratch—and reaching the goal of not knowing and yet experiencing everything.

Temples in India were dedicated and built for saints who reached this ultimate state called Samadhi, Nirvana, Liberation, and some even left their bodies trying to achieve it. My mother told me stories about saints who were dedicated and determined to arrive at this internal peace and how they made it. This realisation of oneself, in turn, is transmitted to others and creates a world of peace.

I was fascinated by these stories and could not imagine that some would bury themselves alive through deep meditation to reach this extraordinary state of peace. I mean, what is this state? Why is it so great that you give up your life for it? You give up everything for this internal peace? Is it that amazing? This state of immortality, I mean, is that even possible? Can we arrive at this state alive too? You usually want to live forever. But you die to live forever? Really?

These saints were extraordinary. They were from all walks of life. Some were kings, and some were princes. Others were ordinary individuals, intelligent people. What drove them to do this?

I used to question how someone could attain and exuberate such peace and happiness without any possessions. Was that even possible? Here I was as a child wanting everything in life, and there, I see these people happy and content with possessing nothing.

I soon realised that liberation leads to a state of inner peace! Spirituality was the path to arrive at this tremendous internal peace. Little did I know my future was built on this realisation of truth!

Summary: I saw my spiritual self while growing up, but only in my reflection. Spirituality was central to my consciousness when I was young, and later I realised that I was a spiritual being. We are all here with a purpose, and mine seems to be the spiritual life. To live with peace and share peace.

What did you see growing up?
What was your conscious experience growing up?
What do you see as your purpose, and how do you manifest it?

Answers:...

Chapter 2

Growing Up With Values

I was born in a small town called Gubbi, around 90 kilometres from Bangalore city. Gubbi is famous for the Sri Channabasaveshwara Swamy temple, where he attained samadhi—a state of joyful calm and rapture—at the age of twenty-five. The temple faces east, and a large lake ripples in front of the temple. Thousands of worshippers visit this temple every day; devotees arriving from all parts of the country take a dip in the holy waters. These sacred waters absolve worshippers for their sins and impurities.

Our family tradition was to visit this beautifully decorated temple, resounding with beautiful chants, and carry out the necessary duties every week. My parents were strict devotees and followed each required tradition. The story of Saint Channabasaveshwara Swamy attaining samadhi by burying himself struck me profoundly. To this day, he could have been one of the primary inspirations for my spiritual growth. My first interest in spirituality was born here. The clear path to samadhi formed when I was five.

My great-grandfather was well known in Gubbi. Throughout his life, he worked diligently and created wealth.

He was kind and generous and was well known and popular in town. My dad, who deeply admired him, talked to me about his granddad's accomplishments and disciplined life endlessly.

Dad told me how his grandpa opened many schools for the poor, built free marriage halls, and provided free meals for the needy; he treated the people of his town, this large community, as his family and helped them develop, and he received a gold medal for his charity. He was truly inspiring. I was fascinated by the stories of how trustworthy and admirable he was. These exemplary accomplishments showed me how to be generous and loving with people.

Being a member of a popular family living in his shadow was exhilarating. Our family received love and respect wherever we went in town. We were recognised as his great-grandchildren and given tremendous attention and care. My brother and I enjoyed the generosity and love of every person in town.

Growing up, we had nothing to complain about, and we were blessed with everything. Everyone around us spoke about our great-grandfather and thanked us for improving our town and community. I quickly realised that the action of good deeds remains longer than one's life. People love people who help others. We are all on this journey of life together. My first impression of being helpful and generous came from him. We never realise where our best qualities come from, and it seems to be from our ancestors.

As I enjoyed this popularity, love, and respect from everyone around me, I soon realised it came with a cost—a set of restrictions. When you are from a well-known family, you must safeguard your family reputation. The pressure of doing everything right and perfectly is immense. It becomes nearly impossible to live an ordinary life. You feel eyes on you from all directions. Can I do this or not? Is this right or wrong? Is it acceptable or not? Is anyone watching me? Is someone judging me? You have to weigh so many questions before you carry out a single action.

Learning ceases because you have a family rulebook repeated every day. You never get to discover for yourself what is right or what is suitable. You followed whatever was taught as good, the best, and right.

Growing up, my father taught me so much. Each morning he read a thought for the day and explained what it meant. I was only five and already learning life lessons. He explained what is right, what is helpful, and what is harmful. He shared many incidences in life and how to overcome life's challenges by following the right path. He saw things clearly, and he taught me how to do that. I developed significant knowledge and clarity through his stories and experiences in life. He could see through people, and he showed me how to observe that. He showed me the meaning of honesty, kindness, punctuality, and loyalty. He lived a life of truth and was a perfect example for me as I grew up.

On the other hand, my mother showed me love and taught me how to love others. She is a deeply religious person and worshipped many gods and goddesses. She went to temples every day, wishing a better life for our family and friends. She met with many astrologists and asked them how to improve our family's fate. How could we resolve upcoming issues? She loved others through her daily prayers and devotion. She went the extra length to help everyone, and through her, I learned to help others unconditionally.

She showed me unconditional love, and this love is what I have learnt to show to others and myself. She showed what love can do in this world and how it can conquer many of life's challenges and hurdles. My brother and I were fortunate to have experienced such genuine love and always felt complete, filled, and happy; she was our rock, our enrichment.

Summary: This spiritual knowledge and love from my father and mother helped me realise life values. Love and light were the solid foundation of my upbringing. I am incredibly grateful for my childhood experiences, and hence I have developed the ability to pass love and light on to others in life.

Can you remember the values held by your family when you were a child?
What influence did they have on you?
How do you utilise those values in your current daily life?
How do you help others through those values?

Answers:...

Chapter 3

Disciplined Life

My dad is disciplined and a self-taught man. His parents never got involved in his upbringing and gave him complete freedom to discover his own. He had the freedom to live the life he wanted. He learned many things from his own life experiences and many people he visited and met while growing up. He had the ability to learn quickly and precisely from anyone he met. From a young age, he had the intellect to distinguish right from wrong and good from harmful.

For example, he woke us at seven every morning and prompted us to get up from the bed's right side as a sign of good omen. He'd then ensure our beds were made, that we were clean, and wearing fresh clothes. We had to say our prayers and do morning exercises. Then he read the thought for the day and asked questions about it, leading to an in-depth discussion about life.

If he ever saw me get big-headed, he immediately dissolved my ego. He taught me about great people's behaviour and how they struggled or behaved in a superhuman manner; he inspired me to be a better human being every day.

I also went to school, came home and changed, then helped my mother with the housework. After dinner came evening prayers. My father taught my brother and me the life skills and knowledge to deal with any situation life could throw at us. He wanted me to be an all-rounder—someone who could help people, have robust life skills, and at the same time look after oneself and be happy.

He also had a gift to teach people anything he learned. Since I was his first child, he wanted to pass on whatever he had learned. When I was quite young, he taught me how to look after my emotions through healing others, to look after my body through yoga, and to look after my mind through meditation.

He showed me how to speak to elders with respect, love the youth for their innocence, appreciate life as it comes, and be a great listener to everyone. He also taught me how to respect myself, hold myself high, and try my best with every-thing I do. He sent me to classes to learn various things like classical dance, music, shorthand writing, computer skills, sports, art, and cooking.

By the time I was twelve, I had developed many skills and an understanding of life. He taught me how to look inwards and be self-aware. He taught me that living a life of hon-esty and truth was most important rather than accumulating wealth, popularity, success, or anything else in life.

Even though living a disciplined life was a formidable challenge to bear at a tender age, it paid off when I got older. Even though I did not always enjoy his teachings and wanted to be free and live my life like other teenagers, I could see the benefit of what he taught. Sometimes I felt unhappy and trapped into the confines of right and wrong. Sometimes I thought these rules were irrelevant. Yet, I knew he only wanted the best for me, and I am incredibly thankful for all the time he spent teaching me self-discipline.

Summary: Living a disciplined life is tough; it requires effort, dedication, and time. However, I know this effort has helped me become self-aware and look after myself well. These lessons have guarded me throughout life; they've helped me fine-tune my emotions, maintain my physical and mental state, and have been a pillar of my life.

How did you develop self-discipline?
Was it challenging to practise it in your life?
How has it helped you shape your life now?

Answers:...

Chapter 4

Experiencing Emptiness

While growing up, I experienced most of the beautiful things I ever wanted to, which left me with a sense of emptiness as I aged. I was not sure at the time what this feeling of emptiness was. It was similar to boredom. In some ways, I felt I'd done what I needed to do, shared what I needed to share, so what else remained? I felt left with a vast void.

The state of void or emptiness began to creep in when I was around thirteen or fourteen. At that time, I ignored that feeling entirely and continued to look for more things to do and more things to experience. Since I was restricted to meeting friends and could not hang out or socialise, I had only a few things to do, unlike other teenagers.

This sense of emptiness enters when you have nothing on your schedule. Most of the time, we usually ignore this void and immediately grab something else to do. But, I invite you to stay with this void and see what happens. Watch your reaction to it. See your behaviour towards it. What do you notice?

Something reveals itself during this void. It is your true self. You begin to see who you are in this emptiness. Try and expand this emptiness so you can see yourself more. We generally bury our true selves with mundane actions, emotions, and thinking. But when all actions or need for actions melt away, you discover your true self.

This nothingness is what we aspire to experience. Tremendous value arises when we experience ourselves. But our minds are uneasy with this practise and immediately try to fill this gap with more thoughts, emotions, or physical activity. This void is a place of creation where authentic creativity happens in life.

Innovation and expertise happen within this void. This empty space seems to encompass the process of birth, living, and death. When I became conscious of this cycle, I gained a more profound clarity on how things originated and how things ended.

For example, I desired a beautiful piece of jewellery and hoped to get it for my birthday. When I received it, I loved it, but immediately after that, I experienced a state of emptiness—the state of nothingness that creeps in immediately after having it.

This was the exact same sensation I felt when I wanted to be first in the class—I worked hard to achieve it, but after earning the best marks, I immediately felt a sense of emptiness. I dove deeply into this emptiness and explored what it was.

Why, after every great experience, did I have this feeling of emptiness? I then realised this is the circle of creation, life, and death. It was happening within multiple dimensions of the Universe. I developed the *Empty Through Living Practise*, which I discuss later, based on this life cycle; I experienced it time and time again.

During my teenage years, I was housebound as my father did not want me corrupted by the outside world. He tried to bring me up perfectly, and he did not wish his teachings and discipline wasted. I did not meet many new people or go out much with friends, and this lack of interaction with others caused a lack of understanding of the world's experience and knowledge.

I was left with much time on my hands to explore within. As I could not explore much outside of me, I dived deeply into myself.

This secluded life kept my mind clear and unconditioned by external influences. Having no choice but to spend lots of time with my thoughts and no outside knowledge to influence me, I discovered pure clarity of my mind. This clarity sustained me and propelled me to see most things in their proper form, without any preconceptions or knowledge of them. This quiet and clear mind developed due to emptying all actions, and later in life led me to create the *Power Flow Practise.*

My empty mind was clear, with no cluttered thoughts. I was free to observe whatever was in front of me with no externally influenced knowledge or identification of any kind. I did not know the world's language; I did not have the world's pressure, and I did not have the labels spoken of the earth. The unconditioned mind develops the ability to see things the way they are without any corruption.

Usually, the outside world corrupts original thinking by dictating right and wrong according to years of other peoples' knowledge. Even though entertaining and exciting to read and learn, this accumulated knowledge of the world slowly corrupts your thinking process. I was lucky enough to get away from all this.

Summary: Experiencing emptiness helped me create a gap between my body and mind. This gap helped me clear my old beliefs, dogmas, judgments, and attachments to see the world anew. Feelings of emptiness can occur when going through extreme life situations like losing a loved one, drastic life changes, severe health issues, and many more.

Have you ever experienced emptiness in your life?
What happened after you experienced it?
What actions did you take, and how did they help you in
      your growth?

Answers:...

Chapter 5

Running Away From It All

Growing up In India, for me, was exceedingly difficult. As unique as it was with all the diversity around me, I grew up with a sense of watchfulness. My parents strictly monitored me, but somehow, I felt like everyone around me also scanned me continuously and checked on me.

I did not realise then that it was my true self witnessing me. Instead, I thought it was everyone else. I felt trapped and not free.

Everything around me offered information on how to live life. As I began to see spirituality around me and learn of various religions directing me to live a conscious life, my family's constant teachings became too much for me.

For example, at one time in my life, I'd attend a wedding. I knew in advance who I needed to speak with to have the proper conversation; I could not talk to anyone I wished. This constant watching of myself to be fair, suitable, and perfect would not leave me alone.

If I spoke to my cousins, they'd encourage me to sneak away behind my parent's back to go with them to get ice cream—this was a colossal crime for me. If they said, "Let's play card games and drink coke," I would be terrified, as I knew my parents deemed that behaviour unacceptable. I could not get involved, so I had to find someone else to talk to and leave that group. This constant pressure of finding the right people to chat with nearly drove me insane. I ended up spending time on my own rather than be wrong.

I felt as if someone regularly watched me to see if I behaved righteously. I was desperate to run away from it all and be free of this watching. I wanted to live a life of freedom. When I attended university, I managed to see and live a little bit of my own life, but I felt like something was still watching me and monitoring me.

I did not realise that no one else actually monitored me, but I subconsciously wanted to live this life of truth. However, my true self guarded me and directed me from a noticeably young age until I was old enough to be liberated. I repeatedly blamed everyone around me for bothering me too much, but, in fact, it was not anyone else. It was my true self.

I did not enjoy university as I was not keen on becoming a dentist, which I studied for. At university, everyone was into their career, wanted to become something, achieve something, and become successful or at least enjoy their lives while they were there, but I was lost. I did not know who else I needed to become or in what field I wanted to succeed.

It was like I knew nothing. Everyone else seemed to know very clearly who they were, what they wanted to be, and how to follow their dream. With my true self always watching, I felt like I needed to run away. I felt suffocated inside my body, and I wanted to run away from everything around me.

While I was at university, my parents arranged for me to meet my husband; he was from England. We met, he liked me just the way I was and promised to look after me. He wanted me to be free. He offered me the freedom I looked for in life. I immediately loved his courage, his honesty, and his capacity to accept me just as I was. I immediately agreed to the match, decided to get married, and flew to England. I thank my husband from the bottom of my heart for giving me this opportunity to live a free life.

Summary: I realise now that I could not run away from my true self; it is ever-present from a young age. I can be free from my true self, consciousness, and be liberated only by embracing myself and living it completely first but not by escaping from it.

What were you conscious of while growing up?
What did you not like about it?
Did you want to be free from your true self too?
Are you free now?

Answers:...

Chapter 6

Knowing Nothing

Arriving in England, I experienced a state where every attachment to past experiences evaporated—twenty years of learned knowledge, emotions, habits, and routines dissolved in the flick of a second. I did not know who I was anymore. I could not identify myself with anything of the past. I felt as though I was born anew. This vast space inside of me opened, and I did not know what it was. It felt empty. There was nothing inside of me.

I felt free but, at the same time, sensed nothing to hold onto. I thought I was flying high and needed to be grounded. But no relationships or attachments had yet developed, and at this point, everything here was new. I began filling this void with various new identities, but no matter how hard I tried, I barely succeeded. The newness in my life was more significant than my ego. The reality overtook me. I had no choice but to go with life.

As I was new to England and did not know anything, I learned everything from scratch. I almost felt like I was a five-year-old. I felt like I knew nothing at all. I spoke English, but I did not understand British English. I could not understand the accent; I could not understand the idea or meaning of what they were saying to me. It was a huge change that I had never expected.

I was born again in England to relearn everything about life. The only thing that stayed with me from India was my awareness. My consciousness level had to increase to a greater degree to understand everything happening around me. Consciousness was the only continuous thing present from India to England. The spiritual me. I now look back to see that the truth remains—the real continues. The true self never leaves you.

I met my husband only a couple of times before we married. I'd never been away from my family and had no close friends or relatives. I lived from the very core of me. However, I was excited and looked forward to experiencing this entirely new life. I had total freedom. No one would tell me to do something this way or that way. No one watched over my shoulders to see if I did right or wrong—no one set any rules, and I felt like a child in Candyland.

I was free to explore my life. I enjoyed waking in the morning and riding the bus to explore my town. I loved observing everything about everyone. I knew nothing. I didn't know who I was, what I was into, what I should understand, or where my life should go. It felt as though my old life had stopped, and all possibility was available to me. I finally opened my eyes and had come out of my body, leading to awakening.

It was as though I left my body in India, and when I came to England, I entered my mind. My body and all its attachments and longings ended—all the previous attachments to the lovely food, the beautiful weather, close family, precious memories, and friends in India had all gone.

Creating a considerable distance from my body helped me explore my mind.

For example, I would wake up and did not know what to do. I had no responsibilities. I ate breakfast and hopped on the bus, riding without a destination. On my first bus ride, I didn't know where to put the money or what notes to use. Since I didn't have a destination, I'd simply tell the driver that I'd ride to the last stop, please. At the last stop, I'd disembark, walk around the place, exploring everything to learn what I could; then, I'd get back on the bus and ride home. My life had no goals; I had no ambition, no end game, no tasks to complete. I was living a life of complete freedom.

Summary: Knowing nothing is what I experienced after awakening. When I jumped out of my body, I began to enter my mind. This positive state of not knowing anything was the first step towards discovering my mind. Cleared of previous attachments to bodily needs, I saw life anew. We all seem to be scared of this state of not knowing. However, the real discovery of truth happens here; otherwise, we simply repeat what we already know.

Have you experienced this state of not knowing in any situation?
How did you deal with it?
What support did you look for during that time?
Did you witness anything new?

Answers:...

Chapter 7

Accumulating Knowledge

Knowing nothing is a perfect place to start exploring the mind. To do this, we need to create a considerable gap between our body and mind. The body instinctively seeks what it loves. Pleasing the body is a tiring job. By creating detachment from our body's desires, we can awaken and step out of the body.

As a child, I never really understood wisdom. Though my dad taught me things, and I learnt other things from the schoolbooks growing up, genuine knowledge of life was something I had not come across. As an adult, I was fascinated. I began to learn about life in broader terms rather than being told what to do, who to speak to, and what to learn.

I began exploring knowledge with a broader mind. I hungered for in-depth knowledge to fill my soul, my interior emptiness. By eating food, we fulfil our body's needs; by reading and accumulating knowledge, we please our mind; through our love for the world and everyone in it, we serve the heart. However, sustaining our soul is our primary purpose. But how do we do this?

These were the thoughts I used to ponder daily. I began to question myself and my actions deeply, attempting to find answers and meaning for myself. During this time, I developed a practise called the *Essence of Questioning*. This practise helped me go deep within myself to find what food serves my soul; it helped me uncover my life's purpose.

Once you begin to step away from the knowledge you've already learned, you can start to explore your mind. You become open to the various options that come your way. You have an entire new library of knowledge to study. You are entering the bank of expertise.

Not knowing who I was or what my purpose was, I started to discover myself. My exploration led me to my first book on spirituality, *The Art of Happiness,* by Dalai Lama—a simple book that explained what happiness was. Even though I did not know what I was looking for, I knew I wanted to be happy. But what is happiness? How do you define happiness? What exactly does happiness mean? Is happiness the result, or is it at the beginning of every action? What do you need to do to get happy? These were all the simple questions so clearly answered in this book.

When I read this book, it was as if I'd found a key that opened the door to the bank of knowledge. I had never known or heard of this book before, yet it connected to everything I knew of spirituality from my childhood.

The spiritual people I used to see in India and hear about elsewhere understood something about the spiritual process. They chose a path to arrive at peace. The Dalai Lama's book was a connecting dot for me. I read the book repeatedly to understand it profoundly and practise what he was saying. I did not know the right way or the wrong way but was determined to grow and fill my soul. I did not understand why I had to do this, but some part of me genuinely wanted to experience this happiness.

One book led to another, and I was soon practising and reading various books on spirituality. I did not understand everything I read, but I knew I connected to it, and I could see the truth. Everything the authors said made clear sense. I implemented all their ideas, trying, testing, and experimenting with every single technique they mentioned. I wanted to discover the truth for myself. I did not just believe it but wanted to verify it and experience it first-hand.

During this chapter of my life, I read books written by J Krishnamurti and Edward Jones. I also read the teachings of Gautama Buddha. I read other books written by different philosophers, thinkers, and scientists. Learning and gathering information was my passion.

My mind was thirsty and wanted to accumulate as much knowledge as it possibly could. This knowledge accumulation did not end. I must have read hundreds of books on various topics and still could not satisfy my thirst for knowledge. Eventually, towards the end of all this learning came the questions, "What am I searching for? What is all this knowledge? Why am I accumulating all this knowledge? What is the benefit of it?"

Was this mental entertainment? Was this to fill my boredom? Or was this to inflate my ego, allowing me to have a great debate or a striking argument? What does it all mean? Ultimately, I realised that seeking knowledge is not truth; rather, the truth comes through experiencing life. I noticed that learning alone could not define the truth; I had to *feel* it and experience for myself the wisdom I'd read. I had to come out of my mind to experience simplicity.

Summary: When I entered the mind's territory, I realised that knowledge is the food. Like the body needs food to live, the mind needs knowledge. When we need food, we eat, but if we overeat, we feel sick, so it goes with the mind. Awareness of our mental needs requires intelligence. By accumulating too much knowledge, I realised I had gone overboard. This excess knowledge becomes waste and needs to be released; otherwise, it builds pressure and causes mental illness.

Have you ever been thirsty for knowledge?
Have you ever been satisfied by feeding your hunger for
    knowledge?
How do you deal with the mental waste?

Answers:..

Chapter 8

Wanting It All

When you are in your twenties, you aspire to live a full life; everything appears beautiful. You seem to enjoy everything; you seem to want everything. You desire to make your body attractive, accumulate knowledge, and wish and aspire to be as loving and peaceful as Buddha.

We misunderstand wanting it all as greedy or ambitious, yet ambition is only a smaller version of reaching unlimited power's ultimate goal. The spiritual journey is concentric; it has many cycles and multiple discoveries before reaching life's ultimate goal. Wanting it all is a smaller version of material omnipotence.

It is almost like a child wishing to have all the toys in the shop. Everything in the world appears beautiful, and hence the inclination to possess everything only seems natural. To become one with everything is what we seem to desire. Yet, we do not know how to become one with everything.

Since it is impossible to be superficially one with objects, we need to turn inwards to realise the ultimate power in everything. This dissatisfaction with not achieving peace from outward possessions indicates the possibility that materialism is not the path to peace. Through despair and unsatisfactory results, we learn and grow.

For example, as I grew up, I wanted to look beautiful and wear beautiful clothes. I wanted to have the most beautiful body, and I went to the gym, spending hours every day to achieve this perfect body. I wanted to be genuinely knowledgeable and wanted to have the most potent and most in-depth understanding of humankind. I wanted to live in a beautiful home with expensive cars, go on fabulous holidays, and see the world. I wanted to have a good husband, loving children, and amazing parents and friends.

I did achieve all this, and I was delighted to have it all. But then what is next? What is after that? What comes after all your desires? If all your wishes are granted, and you've experienced all life has to offer, what is left? The same empty feeling of nothingness. Without introspection, this emptiness is always present. When you empty yourself through living out your desires, you find the real you. Only the experience and consciousness of who you are brings immense peace.

Summary: I tried to feel omnipotent physically, then mentally, then emotionally, only to realise that true omnipotence arises through subtle states of awareness. I could not accumulate a sense of fulfilling satisfaction physically, mentally, or emotionally from the outside.

The fine quality of the mind is still not practical enough to expand in the galactic dimension. The subtlest quality of feelings is still not the answer. But I soon realised that consciousness is the only quality that can permeate everything and still be present everywhere. Through this quality of awareness, one can expand in this world, the next world, and the entire universe. This awareness can grow and develop until we realise we are indeed this beautiful universe, and we are indeed the omnipotent, but living this human life.

Have you tried to accumulate material things?
What did you experience?
Were you satisfied?
Did you experience oneness with it?

Answers:..

Chapter 9

Finding a Guide

When I began my spiritual search with a desire to discover my purpose, I found no one to contact in England. I wanted to wake up every morning with the desire to understand what life was all about. Yet, I had no one to guide me. Others could teach me the daily routines of ordinary life, but that is not what I sought. I turned to books and a few old videos, but often I could not understand what they were saying or what they meant.

Books offer great information, but it's a one-way conversation. Reading old books and watching old videos facilitate knowledge, but truth is discovered in the now. As we all know, communicating with every generation is a challenging task. My children wonder what I am saying. With every age, we lack proper communication. You can imagine someone discovering a truth years ago then communicating that truth through the language of that time. It's in the past. I was looking for a living Guru or an enlightened master with whom I could have a face-to-face conversation and who could point to the truth in the now.

I looked desperately to find someone who could answer my questions and guide me at this moment. I found a few spiritual beings, but they could not answer many of my questions. They were themselves lost in their search and still discovering. I had hundreds and thousands of questions in my mind which needed answers. Every minute I questioned why it is this way? Which is the path I need to take? Is what I'm doing right? Does this make sense? Am I going insane?

I had to settle for buying and reading more books, watching videos of all the old gurus, philosophers, thinkers, scientists, and spiritual beings I could find on the internet. So much information was available that it became difficult to distinguish between who's telling the truth and who isn't. Many people claimed they were enlightened and transformed, but I had no access to them. I tried to find many of these people online so I could speak with them; however, I rarely found access, and when I did, they never really answered my most profound questions.

My questions mounted daily. Without answers, fully in doubt, not knowing what steps to take next, not knowing which direction to go, I would stay up all night reading everything I could find. Ultimately when I could not find anyone to answer my question, I'd ask the Universe, and it would point me towards certain information, to a specific book, or to a person to give me the answer I sought.

After long searching, I managed to find one person in America named Edward Jones; he was willing to listen to my questions and was ready to be my spiritual friend. We exchanged many emails and kept in contact, discussing questions and answers. These interactive conversations and discussions truly helped me with my spiritual growth.

I realised how having a specific guide genuinely helps spiritual seekers on their spiritual path. I felt a need for a present-moment spiritual teacher or guide—someone who could answer my questions directly. The guide or coach helps people reflect on problems and nudges them to see their inner truth.

Without having the right direction, my path was not easy. I didn't have a guru or guide, and doing all this learning from scratch was an arduous, long, and challenging journey. Being directionless adds extra years to your search for the ultimate truth and delays your arrival. Finding the truly realised guru or a spiritual teacher is significant.

In my search, I found many who called themselves gurus or masters, but they were mainly after fame or money. Inner realisation comes in many forms, but ones who teach only philosophy or theory are best avoided. Completion is an actuality. The guru should be living a life of truth, not just philosophising or theorising about it. Only when you live your truth are you realised.

Awareness of the false teachers is crucial in your journey. Because you are in a vulnerable state, some false teachers try to steer your path away from realisation and make you believe in something untrue. You are open; you want to learn and develop genuinely. If you progress intellectually, but not in real life, that would be of concern. Knowledge is only one aspect of inner knowing. The right guru shows you to live the truth. Following your intuition about finding the right teacher is crucial. Ultimately you are your own guru.

Be patient with yourself. During my spiritual quest, I spent a multitude of hours reading, watching videos, meditating, listening to music, and learning through any format possible. The process took several years, used up much energy, offered lots of trial and error. I went forward, sideways, backwards, and in circles to reach where I've reached.

Summary: I believe having a spiritual guide or teacher is essential. A true guide makes your journey smoother and more relevant. Rather than spending years looking to find the right path, a guide or a coach may help make your transformation easier.

Did you ever feel stuck in your spiritual journey?
Did you come across any guide or a mentor who helped you?
Have you been a mentor to anyone looking for help?

Answers:..

Chapter 10

The Family Life

Being spiritual was incredibly challenging, and having a family life was exceedingly difficult. Balancing family life with a husband and kids and wanting to find the true meaning of life is incredibly challenging. Sometimes I felt like I lived a double life. At times I was so dedicated and deeply involved in my spiritual search that I lost track of my family's needs.

By the time I had done my daily tasks and looked after my family, I had no energy left to think about anything else in life. Most of our lives are busy from morning until evening. We work to meet daily demands, which often take over our lives, and little time or energy is left to consider anything else in life.

At one point, my family felt like a burden, and I became distant. I wanted to be left alone in my search, and this created an unhealthy relationship with everyone. I never realised how intensely and deeply focused I was on my quest. Sometimes I forgot where I was, who I was with, and what I was doing.

I heard about spiritual people looking for liberation who would leave their families to go live alone or in the woods. It made clear sense to me, and I felt the urge to do the same. Our daily activities and worldly needs are so demanding, and it is difficult to escape that. I often recalled Lord Buddha's story, where he left his wife and child as he sought the truth. But is this the only way we can find our spiritual reality?

In my case, my family did not know spirituality, nor were they interested in learning about it. Spirituality is not a common thing. Not many people understand it; for some, it appears to be a waste of time seeking the unknown. Everyone likes to see something tangible and factual but running after the impractical seemed like a dumb thing. Hence, my family was not supportive of me as I continued seeking.

Spirituality has many definitions, but in my own experience, I would say it is discovering who you are—in the most profound sense—and finding a way to separate from your attachments to experience yourself fully and become a new being.

Regardless of what anyone in my family said or did, I was focused. I was dedicated and loved what I was doing. I overcame family, personal, and work obstacles by sheer commitment. I saw the results of my progress and its positive effect on my life. I learned endlessly, sought the right knowledge, and did not give up. I practised tirelessly to improve myself and develop into a better human being. I realised my life was not perfect. I was not a perfect human being. I had learnt a lot from many mistakes in life, and now I was open, spoke the truth, and lived a true life. I listened to myself deeply and trusted my intuition. I carried out strict discipline to overcome life's obstacles.

I was intensely focused, and it almost came to a point where my family did not want me to continue my spiritual search. They thought I was going crazy. I talked about it and explained to them about life and spirituality, and eventually, they stopped listening. I reached a point where I decided to leave them and seek the ultimate truth. I left my family and went to live by myself. Nobody was ready to accept the way I was, and I decided living by myself would facilitate my learning.

During this part of my journey, I questioned my every thought and action. I began to see traces of reality opening to me and would spend hours in deep observation. It was an effective method of discovering myself at a deeper level. I spent many hours in spiritual practises, which led me to develop a greater understanding and awareness of reality. Reality was opening to me.

Living away from the world's falseness, any attachments I had unfettered, it was as though I had no more ties to this world or my past. I was left free. Once again, a huge gap or space was created, allowing room for something new to happen. It was during this time that I experienced a life-changing event. The incident opened me to see my false self. In that instant, I noticed that I was not the qualities of my father or my mother, who had lived my life so far. I was free from all bondages of life and was left entirely alone.

This experience removed every false identification of me and left me at peace, at the very ground of creation. Creation being the ocean of manifestation. This experience was the final transformation. Initially, I did not appreciate what this experience was. It later dawned on me that this was true enlightenment. I saw my past identifications die and a new being born. This enlightenment gave rise to *The School for*

Enlightenment. The school's intention is to help everyone discover their true self, experience internal peace, and transform into a new being.

After my enlightenment, I continued growing spiritually. I discovered real love, an authentic self, and liberation. I dove into creating the school and began helping others find their true self. Eventually, my family began to admit that I was serious, spiritual, and committed to this journey. Hence, my family agreed to let me live my life the way I wanted, and I decided to re-join them.

The responsibilities that we are born with, or we have in our lives are crucial. Regardless of your involvements or interests, you still need to fulfil your duties; it would help if you still were engaged in life. Separating your spiritual life from your family life or your work life can only make you imbalanced.

As I learned, spirituality was about living your present spiritual life while being involved with everything around you. You need to maintain your responsibilities and help others understand your perspective while accepting their point of view.

Summary: Family life is not easy in itself. But if you genuinely want to find your true self and want to know your purpose in life, you will find a way to balance the whole. I'm an example of blending being a spiritual seeker, having family responsibilities, and still finding my true self. So, it is possible to find genuine spiritual reality without having to sequester yourself.

Have you experienced any difficulty while on a quest for
knowledge?

Have family and friends stood in your way as you searched
for the truth?

How did you overcome those obstacles?

Answers:..

Part 2

Practises to Enlightenment

Chapter 11

Power Flow Practise

What is the Power Flow Practise and How Does It Benefit Life?

The Power Flow Practise helps you completely relax and let go of all tension in your body. Any stress you might have accumulated or any worries over time can be dissolved through this practise. Any longings, any emotions, any addictions you might have can all be reduced and eventually eliminated.

The Power Flow Practise helps you settle your busy mind and encourages your body to relax. By slowing your mind, you can learn to tap into the unlimited energy available to us all. We all have access to this source of infinite power, which may be lying dormant and undiscovered.

Power is unconditioned pure energy, the energy which has not been here before and has a quality of newness. This power is potential energy and helps us see reality more clearly.

The Power Flow Practise is a remarkably simple but effective strategy that can be mastered by anyone. You can start at any time, and you don't need any special tools to put it into practise. Continuous practise of this technique will take you to higher levels of accomplishment in your life.

The benefits of this practise are life-changing, and the effects instantaneous. Learning to access the purest potential energy has many benefits, including creativity, clarity of mind, positivity, high energy, increased mental strength, and a better quality of sleep.

Through this practise, you'll slowly learn to relax your mind, stop your mind, then eventually come out of your mind. You can see the effects within three weeks, and you'll move through the phases of awakening, enlightenment, discovering your true self, and finally, finding liberation. This is a one-stop practise for everything.

How Do You Implement the Power Flow Practise?

The Power Flow Practise is best achieved in a quiet place. A quiet room is helpful as initially, noisiness can interrupt this form of practise. You can also light a candle, if it helps you, to create a calm and serene surrounding. You can play calming music to relax and let go of your body.

Lie down and take a break from everything. When you lie down, close your eyes take a couple of deep breaths, and intentionally stay awake. There's no need to worry about breathing in any particular way, focusing on the third eye, or anything else you may have read about in other practises.

You are completely relaxing—you allow your body to let go, your mind to slow down, your emotions to be what they are, your awareness to be free. There's no restriction, no focusing, no concentrating. You're being rather than doing.

Start with just five minutes a day and add a bit more time daily. If you can, try to do this practise each day at the same time and in the same surroundings; it will slowly make it easier for your body and mind to settle into that state quickly.

Physical Effects During the Power Flow Practise

When you lie down and intentionally stay awake, you will notice sensations start to rise from your feet; the sensations begin to gather and eventually rise to the crown of your head.

Everything happens by itself; you don't need to think, label, or understand anything. If you feel like nothing is happening, that's okay. Just stay with the practise of lying still and remaining awake.

You'll slowly notice the sensations in your legs start to rise and slowly begin to feel the sensations in your hands, in your chest, in your shoulders, in your neck, until they concentrate near your forehead. This process clears all the tension and stress built up in your body that has moved up into your head.

As you continue with this practise, you'll notice that eventually, all your body's accumulated tension feels forced into your forehead. If you find this sensation uncomfortable at first, just continue breathing; the discomfort will pass. Slowly you will see that this force starts to rise above you and move upwards.

When this force rises above your physical body, it's as though somebody's taken away all the tiredness, stress, and tension, bundled it all up and thrown it above you. The body is relaxed, and you have recovered your body from any strain or tension at this point.

Eventually, you will start to see your thoughts clearly once your bodily sensations have died down. Often, thoughts begin to take the place of physical sensations. You are now entering the mind.

Mental and Emotional Effects During the Power Flow Practise

Once your bodily sensations fade and you enter the mind, you'll notice your thoughts. They can be short thoughts or long thoughts; they can be old or new. Again, there is no need to do anything. Just let the thoughts come and go; you don't need to observe anything at all. You need just to stay awake; that's all you have to do in this practise.

Often when you enter the mind, you feel you have no direction. No one stands with a signpost saying this is where you need to go, or this is where you need to turn left or right. Free yourself from expectation, allow your intuition to take over. When you are in this state, you might feel you are not in control, but that is the whole idea behind it: to observe the state of no control of the mind.

Taking care of your mind through the Power Flow Practise is like learning the next level of seeing. By releasing intentional or negative thoughts, we create space for intuitive enlightened visions to enter. We exercise our bodies to stay healthy; this practise is an exercise for our minds.

By staying awake, you consciously overcome your body's sensations and disturb thought patterns of the mind. By staying awake and simply being without thinking, you enter a pure awareness of yourself. You are not engaging your bodily, emotional, or mental needs. This practise helps you face your everyday life through expanded awareness. This increased awareness allows you to deal with life situations with a sense of clarity, peace, and calm.

This practise also helps you to detach from events in life. Emotional detachment doesn't mean that you no longer care; rather, you're able to view events from a place of peace and clear-headedness. As you become skilled with this practise, eventually, you'll find that no matter what comes your way, you'll be able to face it with calm awareness, and you'll find that solutions arise nearly without effort.

The Power Flow Practise helps you reduce confusion in all aspects of life. Where you've been twisted emotionally begins to unwind. Solutions to problems become clearer. You start making effective decisions and start seeing life as it is rather than through your veil of emotional or physical responses and temptations. This power you develop is the real power to overcome anything in life.

As you continue this practise daily, you will experience a sense of focused energy in your forehead. As the energy begins to rise above your body, you'll start seeing a light.

Coming Into the Light

Initially, this light appears faintly, seemingly at a distance. However, as you continue to practise this, slowly building from five minutes to ten minutes, to fifteen, and on to twenty and more, you will come across a bright white light as the weeks and years progress.

This light arrives after the many thoughts in your mind cease. You'll notice this white light seems as though it's flowing over you. It clears all your mental stress. It begins to cleanse you of your built-up emotional struggles and eases your physical pain.

Eventually, with continued practise, you'll float through this white light, going higher and higher, until you discover your heart has been opened. You connect through your heart rather than your mind. This becomes a place where you know you can empty your body's tension, where your emotional and mental stresses dissolve, and where your entire system becomes clean and renewed. You will eventually master to hold your breath to an optimum level by being able to tame the life force in you.

As you clear your accumulated stress and tension over time, you will be able to detach yourself from the unconsciousness. Unconsciousness being the old you. You will discover a new consciousness. When new consciousness meets your breath of life force, you transform into a New Being. This being will expand and rise above to be liberated in life.

The Power Flow Practise was the first practise I developed, and over time it totally liberated my life. I hope you will try this practise and that it liberates your life as well.

How I Discovered the Power Flow Practise

When I moved to England, I felt empty and had few friends. I searched for anything that would fill that sense of emptiness. It was a new feeling to me, and I had difficulty identifying what word to associate with how I felt.

Someone suggested that I try reading books about spirituality. I had nothing to lose, so I followed the advice. Soon I was reading a wide variety of books and watching as many videos as I could. Reading books and watching videos helped me deepen my knowledge, but I still felt unfulfilled and confused, as I did not completely understand what they were trying to convey.

This sense of confusion and unclear direction on how to effectively deepen my spiritual life led to disappointment. At the time, I did not know I was searching for my true self.

At that time in England, not many people were familiar with spirituality, and I could not find quality teachers that I resonated with. I found online meditation that I could practise independently, but I found the techniques being taught were complicated and confusing. Without direct access to a teacher, it was hard to follow anything, and I had no idea where those meditation practises would lead.

Being a wife, mother, and working person, I did not have much time to devote to navigating my mind. However, I knew this learning path was important, and I had to stride ahead. I used to stay up all night, researching, learning, understanding, and experimenting, trying to figure out what spirituality was about.

I could not follow somebody blindly as that was not my personality, and that is not spirituality. In spirituality, you want to experiment and verify everything. Whether it's right or wrong for you, it must be tested on your own, as you cannot simply take someone's word for it. Even though the path was difficult, I was determined to figure it out for myself and see the truth.

Having tried and tested most of the meditation teachings I found on the internet, I still had no luck succeeding at any specific practise. I was totally upset and disappointed. I remember going to bed and lying down and closing my eyes with no hope.

I lay down but stayed awake—after laying on my back for about ten minutes, something extraordinary happened. I observed that I was slowly relaxing. My body felt as if it was sinking to the ground. The thoughts in my mind slowed down, and my emotions dissolved quickly.

I felt a sense of ease, as though I was out of synch with time. I felt as if I were being pulled out of life for a while. It was as if I were totally aware of everything, yet I could experience a deeper part of me. I felt almost as though nothing from this world could touch me anymore. I felt invincible.

That day, I realised I was fully awakened. I was so awake and so energetic that I felt I could deal with anything thrown at me. I was in a state of awe. I had discovered a place of peace and tranquillity. I had found the path to my true self— the inner gates were opened. This was the beginning of my self-realisation. My spiritual path had finally appeared, and I was opened to a new way of being.

I discarded all the meditation and yoga practises that had confused me and decided to pursue my own path to inner peace. Every day I found time to lie down on my bed and close my eyes, relax and stay awake as long as I could. This was a simple, doable, and effective practise.

I would practise just lying there and being relaxed and awake. I started with five minutes, then shifted to ten, and eventually practised this technique for twenty minutes each day. Finally, over a few months and years, I slowly increased the length of this practise to as long as two hours per day.

After practicing this for about two years, I came to call it Power Flow Practise because this technique gave me immense power to cope with life—to deal with whatever was thrown at me. It helped me navigate through life, through my mind, and deal with everything that was coming my way. I now had an enormous amount of confidence to face life. This practise was a time out from a busy, hectic, noisy, and overwhelming life. I found an escape route!

During Power Flow Practise, life stopped for me. If you go out for a walk, to the gym, have lunch with friends, watch TV, or read a book, you can relax, but you cannot pause your life. You cannot take a break from it. You cannot sort out the previous accumulations or issues. But through this practise, you create a gap—a gap that helps you come out of this busy life, busy mind, or everyday craziness. It's almost a reset button that you can press when you need to recharge yourself.

Chapter 12

Empty Through Living Practise

In this Empty Through Living Practise, you will learn how to awaken from unhealthy or excessive physical attachments, ranging from a flavour you'd like to taste, a workout plan you'd like to follow, a soothing sensation you can't live without, to deep desires and addictions.

You'll learn how to end bodily entanglements and minimise the amount of control your body has over your day-to-day life. This practise will help you bring your deep desires to the surface, to understand what drives them. You'll begin to free your body as if emptying it from these desires.

How Does the Empty Through Living Practise Work?

Over the years, you might have accumulated many physical desires to the point where your body feels like it can no longer breathe. This Empty Through Living Practise helps you to wake from your unconscious and unaware state to a conscious life in this body.

As I deepened my Empty Through Living Practise over the months and years, I noticed a clarity in my life. All my doubts, issues, and troubles slowly ebbed away. As I cleared one layer of self-doubt, another layer revealed itself. Layer after layer rose to the surface until I began to discover my deepest self.

As self-doubt rose to the surface in waves and layers, I realised that other desires and attachments arose as well. I had deep attachments to many things, and ultimately, I had to deal with them.

I discovered that the easiest way to deal with most of my deepest desires was to embody those desires and live them. I chose not to hold myself back. I chose to embrace and experience all the desires and wishes that bubbled up. However, I consciously experienced these events with acute awareness.

For example, when I fancied having a nice meal out, I'd book myself a table and invite a friend to join me; sometimes, I'd even eat a wonderful dinner on my own. If I felt like going to the gym, I would go; if I felt like spending an afternoon on the couch watching movies, I would. If I felt like learning something, I'd study.

In this way, big or small, I consciously and with awareness lived out most of my desires.

As you start completing your desires, intentionally savouring each moment, everything underneath starts to surface. Believe me, there's always plenty more underneath. The reason we have so many desires is because we haven't consciously lived them. Once they are lived consciously, they will slowly disappear.

Hence the Empty Through Living Practise will clear your desires one by one and lead you to a more conscious life.

Benefits of the Empty Through Living Practise

Through this practise, you stop accumulating inconsequential desires. As you practise experiencing events and daily life with awareness, you begin to live a more complete life. Everything becomes satisfying, and you move away from the dissatisfaction of wishing for something but not making it happen.

You learn how to detach. Detachment arises when you live out an experience with awareness. Attachment occurs when you wish for something to happen, but you cannot bring it into reality.

As you practise living with awareness and create experiences for your desires, you have fewer unfulfilled desires. You begin to live out your oldest and deepest desires intentionally; you start to Empty Through Living.

Do your best to minimise your need for control over the outcome. Remember to live your life and find peace within yourself. As you enjoy your life and begin exploring these deeper desires, you'll see that what you always wanted to do, what you always longed for, is within your grasp. Do your best to experience the world; go out and live your existing desires in the safest way possible.

When you make this choice, you minimise the nagging thoughts that constantly echo in your head. Taking action on your desires ultimately leads to detachment from them. Your mind is no longer filled with daydreams.

Remaining stuck in a cycle of daydreaming is the reason your desires and longings are not fulfilled. All you're doing is imagining it; you're not taking action. Turning these daydreams into lived events is the best way to empty ourselves and keep ourselves new, uncluttered, and fresh all the time.

Through this Empty Through Living Practise, you discover how to live your life by letting go of your physical attachments towards your deep desires, past memories, and unfulfilled actions. You only have to experience everything once consciously, then the hunger for the same experience subsides.

An unlived life with an accumulation of desires may cause you to become numb and desensitised to your reality. Emotional responses to imagined life experiences keep you bonded to them. Emotional attachment—either positive or negative emotions—blinds you from seeing the reality of life.

This Empty Through Living Practise can be done anytime and anywhere. This practise has many benefits, some of which include overcoming unpleasant habits, addictions, abuse of self and others, and freeing you from being burdened by heavy emotions. In effect, the Empty Through Living Practise may help you feel unattached, grounded, relaxed, and free.

How the Empty Through Living Practise Came to Be

Growing up, I had many desires and dreams. I wanted to buy certain clothes, watches, shoes, go on holidays, buy nice cars, etc. My desires seemed to have no end. I noticed that with so many desires and dreams and wishes to conquer the world, how can I ever live happily?

Do we die being unfulfilled? Is there a way to fulfil all our dreams and desires, then we can be at peace? I always wondered that.

Then I began to wonder, what if I can't afford all that I want to experience? I had to fulfil my desires more smartly. I was not the one who controlled my desires; the more I exerted control, the more I wanted something. I had to be financially smarter. I realised that my desire didn't know how expensive something was; it just wanted to experience it. So, for expensive experiences, I tried to make them small. As long as you experience it, whether for a few days, one hour, or ten minutes, the being that drove the desire has experienced it. So I always found a smarter way to fulfil my dreams and desires and completed them fully. This gave me tremendous peace and let me be free.

Chapter 13

The Essence of Questioning Practise

In this Essence of Questioning Practise, we will teach our minds to question everything. You will attempt to avoid taking for granted all you've been taught, what you've observed or read. You will, as if with an innocent mind, question your beliefs and years of unverified thinking.

This practise encourages you to question everything. We reach deeply into our roots and the darkest corners of our minds and hearts and pull everything into the light.

If we're angry, we question why we are angry. If we behave a certain way, we explore what caused us to behave like that. We reflect on what factors were involved. We wonder, "Who is this person acting in this fashion; am I acting from my true self or as guided by the teachings of someone else?"

If we're happy, are we happy because somebody else would be happy in such a situation? Or are we genuinely delighted because we see the beauty in front of us?

The Essence of Questioning Practise teaches our mind to question everything rather than accept anything blindly. It teaches us not to simply follow something just because it appears good, enjoyable, or happy.

How the Essence of Questioning Practise Came to Be

As my meditation practise evolved and grew, I worked with the Power Flow Practise and the Empty Through Living Practise. I continuously attempted to pursue detachment and began to unload years of accumulated mental, emotional, and physical baggage.

While intentionally living these two practises, I added a new element. I started to question my every action.

Before this awakening, most of my actions were unconscious, involuntary, and reactive. If you take a clear look at your life, you'll notice most of your actions are not conscious; it's almost like your actions are reactions to other responses.

It seems as if we've been trained from a very young age to behave in certain ways. We're taught, when situation A arises, reaction B is the appropriate response. We begin to develop routines and abandon variation.

When I was juggling a job, raising two kids, and managing many other life requirements, I easily fell into unconscious routines. I was exhausted, and the thoughtless patterns made it easier to make it through each day. Sometimes I'd think about switching things up, but I couldn't seem to enact change. I then felt guilty for wanting to create any new life patterns, so I gave up and fell back into the rut.

Your mind will tell you that you haven't done enough, that you're not good enough, that you haven't reached your capacity, and you still have so much more to do. Your mind asks, "Why isn't that finished? Why isn't this finished? Why is that project incomplete?"

Your mind and its routines begin to take on a form of authority and control; it's like working for a narcissist. You almost feel bullied by all the tasks your mind wants you to do. Often it asks too much.

To appease the mind, we become so used to our routines that we cannot live without them. I had a strict daily routine that I followed for many years. If I didn't follow it, or if one part of it was out of place, I would panic. I would feel unsettled and would be convinced that something in the day would go wrong. My mindset and outlook for the day were corrupted.

I bet many of you have routines like this. You may do everything possible to keep this routine going. Whether it makes sense or not, whether we have enough time for this routine or not, we've been told that the mind needs routine.

Somehow, we feel our day has to follow this consistent path to ensure our lives are more at ease.

However, often we don't question why we follow this routine. Rarely do we ask, "What happens if I don't do this? Am I such a robot that all these actions must take place for me to maintain a positive mindset?"

Embodying the Essence of Questioning Practise

Have you ever questioned your old routines? Have you ever wondered why you get up on the same side of the bed every day or why you eat a particular breakfast daily? Have you ever questioned why you wear certain clothes every day or why you go to the gym every day? These routines don't seem to have any connection, yet in reality, we've adopted them, and our unconscious mind has taken control.

We've not cultivated the ability to question ourselves and our habits. We simply follow the patterns the mind has built for us over the years. The mind seems to have taken over our free will and tells us what should be done or not done. We will go the extra length, the extra mile, to please the mind.

The Essence of Questioning Practise helps you overcome these routines. It enables you to expand beyond your current limitations. You develop the strength to ask your mind, "Why do I have to do this? Why does it have to be done this way?"

This questioning of every action helps you develop a certain intelligence, which is useful in seeing the truth rather than simply reacting as if on autopilot.

In this practise, you question yourself deeply. You intentionally reflect on all of your thoughts and actions. This, in turn, leads to deeper insights. Ultimately, this practise helps you see the truth and evaluate your judgments, beliefs, and opinions more clearly.

We don't notice it, but our minds rarely tell us we're doing well, that we've done enough, that it's time to rest. Instead, our minds continually ask us to do more.

However, once you learn the Power Flow Practise and learn to Empty Through Living, you have more energy, clarity, and awareness so you can really see your actions clearly.

In the Essence of Questioning Practise, you ask yourself, "Why am I doing all this cleaning? Who's actually going to judge whether or not the kitchen is spotless? Who will tell me the shelves are not dusted perfectly?"

In some cases, you may diet until you nearly die, but who are you trying to please? In other cases, you may try to accomplish fifteen tasks before you rest for the night when in reality doing seven today and the rest tomorrow may be good enough.

The Essence of Questioning Practise helps you recognise that you can free yourself from self-judgement.

By questioning the very root of a problem, you will become closer to your true nature and discover new intelligence.

Benefits of the Essence of Questioning Practise

As you gain more and more awareness and clarity, you begin to question each of your actions. This questioning allows the bubbling up of a certain remarkable form of intelligence.

This intelligence that arises through questioning your actions is the truth. It is the real truth that allows you to see that your circumstances are not as you imagined them to be; instead, you begin to see the reality of life without the filters of old patterns. You see the real truth of life.

As more and more wise intelligence arises from your questioning, you begin to observe your life's essential truth.

This Essence of Questioning practise can be done anytime and anywhere. It is particularly useful for busy people as it does not require a special place or time to carry it out. You will benefit immensely from overcoming many of your self-imposed restrictions in life.

The benefits of this practise include deconditioning years of unverified knowledge and patterns from your mind, deeper insight, personal freedom, a clearer understanding of life's nuances, increased wisdom, and higher intelligence.

Chapter 14

Observing the Truth Practise

The Observing the Truth Practise is done when you've finished questioning everything and when you start to see the truth for yourself rather than take anything for granted.

Now that you've worked with the Essence of Questioning Practise, you're ready for the Observing the Truth Practise. To observe the truth, you must detach from the trappings of the mind.

The mind is a maze of thoughts, beliefs, dogmas, and wrong-thinking. Only through observing what is happening to you and around you can you discover the truth. Only then can you come out of that mind-maze and walk toward enlightenment.

When you question everything, you will hear a certain intelligence providing answers. This intuitive intelligence speaks to you from the depths of its wisdom and reveals the truth. This practise takes patience. Be kind to yourself in the process.

How to Activate the Observing the Truth Practise

Begin moving away from the reliance on books or other information resources to answer your questions. Instead, spend time sitting quietly with yourself. Intelligence is gained through observation and through listening to your inner-self.

For example, if you want to learn about a tree, rather than find a book about it, spend time loving it and observing it. Look closely at the tree and notice its movements, its colour, the smell of the bark. Imagine talking with the tree and observe its intelligence in its reactions and communication with you. This is real learning about someone or something in the present moment. This is an example of Observing the Truth Practise.

You're learning for yourself from scratch and not relying on input from others. This is your first-hand truth through experience. The Observing the Truth Practise does not apply solely to learning about the physical world. It can be used for mental, emotional, and spiritual learning as well.

Let's look at another example. Imagine a situation where someone has emotionally hurt you. Do your best to recall the circumstances accurately so you can observe wisely. Imagine your daughter calling you and saying, "Mom, I hate you." Observe what's just happened.

Normally we react immediately based on whatever we've learned or been taught in our life. Sometimes that prevents us from seeing the real truth of the matter. Instead, observe your pain without reacting. Explore why you feel this pain. Is it because you are overly attached to your daughter, perhaps emotionally dependent on her for love and attention?

If this is the case, and you see it when you follow the Observing the Truth Practise, you recognise this sense of being emotionally hurt is inevitable. However, you also realise you are emotionally attached and can begin working to detach yourself from her emotionally.

From this new perspective, when you continue to observe your reactions during your conversation with her, you begin to see how emotionally heavy your attachment to her had been, and now you begin to feel lighter.

You used to feel emotionally controlled by her words, expression of feelings, actions, gestures, and so on. But by observing the truth of the situation, you're learning about yourself, and you're learning about your relationship with her.

Here's another example. If you respond in a particular way when your husband comes home, old patterns cause this behaviour. The next time he comes home, observe your thoughts and how your body reacts. Notice how you hold yourself and how you respond to his words and presence.

You might be emotionally attached to particular ideas of him, or you might have a certain image of him in your head but without knowing that you react a certain way. The Observing the Truth Practise helps you begin to see and express yourself clearly, honestly, and truthfully as you let him know what you truly feel and think. By observing the truth and speaking the truth, you start to learn to live in truth, which, in turn, expands your reality.

This practise replaces rumination—that constant thinking of thoughts not based on fact—or denying how you feel. This practise helps you examine your emotions and release emotional baggage. When we don't speak our truth, our emotional layers become heavier and heavier, eventually wearing us down.

As you continue with the Observing the Truth Practise, you begin to see things more clearly, and you can more effectively create positive and healthy changes in your life.

Benefits of the Observing the Truth Practise

Observing the Truth is an effective and uplifting method for dealing with emotions. We begin to see the hidden things we normally gloss over because we're emotionally enmeshed.

Observing the truth takes practise. Because we are so caught up with our emotional distress, we often have difficulty seeing what is happening in stressful situations. The Observing the Truth Practise helps you create and maintain a gap between the situation—or the people involved in the situation—and you. The ability to distance yourself and observe what is happening in front of you offers a tremendous sense of internal wisdom.

This gap is the birth of awareness. This distance and detachment allow us to glimpse reality. As you slowly develop this gap and create space between everything in life, you will enter a detached reality, which is awareness.

This awareness is pure seeing; it's not the seeing of the mind or the reaction of emotions. It is simple, natural, peaceful, clear awareness. This awareness can grow and extend to the level where you will eventually start to live in this state. Observing the truth at all times becomes second nature. When you live in awareness, you can handle any situations that come your way. Your heart opens, and you soften, becoming more loving toward yourself and others.

As you enter this awareness and open your eyes, you'll be able to see others without judgement. You'll be able to connect more easily and peacefully with others. You'll discover your true capacity to give and receive love when you open your heart.

This Observing the Truth Practise can be lived every moment of the day. With patient practise, you'll be able to observe the truth and maintain this distance between yourself and situations. You'll learn to live with detachment and an open heart, both of which help you evolve emotionally and discover your true self. You will develop the art of living with intuitive intelligence.

Though this is an advanced practise, and particularly useful to someone who is already on the path to finding their true self, it is worth the effort. Ultimately this practise helps you develop self-awareness cultivates inner peace, a feeling of connectedness, deep love, and a greater sense of ease and wholeness.

How Observing the Truth Practise Came to Be:

I was caught up in my mind since childhood. I did not interact much outside with many people and did not really enjoy being out. This led me to investigate each and every corner of my inner being. I had plenty of time with myself, and all I ever did was go deep within and explore the ins and outs of myself.

I was watchful of my body, my mind, and my emotions every second. When I was upset, I would go into it to discover the real cause of my distress, and I had to find the solution if I wanted the feeling to stop once and for all.

Once I began exploring, I noticed that we tend to miss the truth. We get so caught up in our minds and in our bodily attachments and obsessions that we miss what has just happened right in front of us. It was by chance that I noticed what was really happening because my mind was quiet.

I saw the truth. Once you see the truth, your thinking and feeling stop immediately. Since then, I started to observe what is happening in front of me, which ended the falseness of the thinking mind.

Part 3

Levels of Being

Being
exists in all levels
Level 5
Liberation
Being
exists as a New Being
Level 4
New consciousness
Being
exists as True Self
Level 3
True love
Being
exists as emotions
Level 2
Enlightenment
Being
exists as the mind
Level 1
Awakening
Being
exists as the body

Chapter 15

Level 1: Awakening

The Body

Typically, we are not fully aware of our body as it mainly operates instinctively. It has many needs, and we spend all day and night fulfilling those needs. We grow up trying to find out its likes and dislikes and satisfy its desires one by one. As we know, our body naturally functions from a young age; we usually are overly attached to it. We keep calling it me, and we point ourselves towards this body. We've entirely connected ourselves and identify ourselves as this body wholly.

Once we learn to understand our body using our mind, we slowly learn to move out of being attached to it. Growing out of or becoming aware of your body to a greater extent is awakening. If this awakening happens consciously, it is conscious awakening; if this happens suddenly, it is accidental awakening. Once you've overcome your major attachments to your body, you then enter the next level of being, which is the mind.

Growing up, we don't know who we are; we're just exposed to or thrown into life. We have a lot to learn, digesting our surroundings, being fascinated about, and getting lost in it all—it can be challenging for every child, teenager, or young adult. Not having enough time to question anything, you go after your attractions, desires, and fascinations. The pressures of the modern world to live a particular way, have certain things, live like everyone else, fit into the community, and do all the things that a normal human being has to do masks our purpose and interest of looking into who one is.

Even though we unconsciously grow up in our teenage years, we have momentary glimpses of who we are. These glimpses of ourselves, a reflection of our true self, are our essence. It's challenging to realise at a tender age in the confusing and overwhelming world what is happening around us and in us. It's as though there's something mysterious about this true self, and it's magical and something you cannot explain.

Glimpses of your true self give you a heightened feeling—the sense of me, a sense of being at home. You always want to return to it without knowing what exactly it is. It is the light of consciousness that you follow to reach your inner self. It's like someone is holding a mirror for you to see your true self in the mirror of consciousness. This conscious seeing is you. You see yourself in a reflection of consciousness. Initially, what appeared as a reflection of you is perceived as outside yourself; you eventually learn to expand and grow into this true self to become one with it.

This search for the true self leads to awakening. When you glimpse it, you are fascinated to the point where you won't enjoy anything else—the taste of your true self is so exhilarating you are lost in search of wanting more. If you have discovered this and see that everything around you is not letting you explore this deepest part of you, you will reach an explosion point. This suffocating feeling of not looking for yourself may cause you to run away. If you cannot do that, life will create a situation for you to get out of your dual state. Life comes to rescue you.

For example, when I started high school in a convent, I was intrigued by the nuns. Why did they wear unique clothes? Why did they isolate themselves from the world? I could not believe that they'd given up everything in their life for something that we don't know much about, God. This experience with the nuns made a big impression on me.

As my passion for spirituality grew each day, I felt like I lived outside of my body. I was living a life that was not mine. By the time I was 18, I knew I had to go to university. At the back of my mind, I knew I could not carry on. With no choice—I had to go ahead with it.

After being in university for two and a half years, I realised that I did not want to be a dentist. I did not enjoy the studies, and I knew it wasn't me. I felt suffocated and restricted.

This question of who I was, was profound and made me restless. I felt I could not stay at university any longer. I needed immense freedom, significant space, and better options to explore my life. The opportunity to go to England was almost a dream come true.

When I moved to England, something inside me opened up like a big void. This empty feeling was unobstructed with nothing in it. It was like a vast space, and something cleared in me and opened up to be freer. It removed all my past attachments to my body and pushed me into another realm that I did not recognise. This led to my awakening. It was like I jumped out of my body into a vast empty mind. This was the action of it, the reality of it.

Awakening is when you begin to turn your focus inward. When most of the body's desires have been fulfilled, and it is happy with itself, you become free from it. The evolution to an inward focus, which is often not apparent, starts to happen from then on. After taking billions of years to develop, the human body—and its instinctive nature—is learning to become conscious of itself now. Becoming aware of oneself seems to be the sole purpose of human development. The first step is to become aware of our body.

Awakening is a wake-up call to start your spiritual journey into who you are. Awakening gives you a slight glimpse of who you might be, and you need to wake up to a bigger reality consciously. When awakened, you feel empowered and energised, and your path laid out to develop further. You experience a shift happening.

In the past, you looked only outwardly, but after awakening, you also start to enquire inwardly. You begin to look inside of you and question everything that is happening. This can be a strange observation initially; however, with time, you gain clarity. You will learn to listen and enquire about what's within you. You open your inner eyes. Awakening opens a path to your true self. It's as though you have moved one step inwards so that you can now not only see the life outside of you clearly, but you also can see your body interacting with the life in front of you. You have gained a deeper view of life. You were looking at your body as an image before, but now you are looking at your body fully present in front of you.

Awakening can happen consciously. Or it may happen unconsciously due to an accident, or due to ill health, having a financial crisis, or any other life-threatening issues. When awakened, you admire what's outside of your body in greater detail. For the first time, you will see your body as a whole, notice the trees around you, the person in front of you, the house you're living, beautiful sunlight, the gorgeous meadows, and the serene life around.

Even though you saw these things before awakening, they look somewhat highlighted and real for you now. It's like they never existed before in this way. Trapped in your body, you couldn't see anything as you were hidden in your eggshell. But now, you slowly start to see the world around you with a better view. It's as though you have used a different lens to see this beautiful life.

When you move inwards, you enter the territory of the mind. You begin questioning everything and dive deeper into your mind. It's as though you are less in your body now and more in your mind. When awakening happens, you also open your third level of being, your emotional layer; this can also be called your heart. We are made of many levels of being, level one being the body, level two being the mind, level three being the emotions, level four being the true self, level five being the new being, and level six of being is existing in all levels.

So, when you are awakened, your major attention shifts from the body to the mind, and a little is moved to the emotional level too. Three functions happen simultaneously, but the percentage of enquiry into each level varies. Hence after awakening, you can feel overwhelmed. Mastering each level is essential to come out of their attachments.

Once awakened, you enter the mind's territory mainly to explore further. This exploration is tremendous and tricky; it's far more significant than understanding the body's strengths and weaknesses. You enter the mind by not knowing much about the mind—how it works, how it functions, what it is about, what tricks it plays, and its many faces.

Information passed down for centuries is stored and locked as knowledge here. Your mind is not solely yours; it is the mind developed for many centuries. This mind has all knowledge; it has many layers and levels to explore.

Entering the territory of the mind is fascinating. You will have a million questions popping into your head. Why is it this way? What is life? What is love? What is the mind? Who is God? What is energy? What is death? And many more.

You want to know about everything. You will start to read an array of books about everything. You are new to this and want to hear from someone already experienced. At this point, you will start to look for a master or a guru. It's almost like you need somebody to show you how to look at things the right way. You've never learned how to see things for yourself but you're learning through somebody else's eyes now.

Imagine you enter the library of mind filled with extensive knowledge by many wise people, and you are just a third-grade student. The mind will eat you up, overwhelm you. You need to learn the alphabet of the mind first, like how you discovered the alphabet of the body when you were three years old. In a similar way, you have to graduate from the library of mind and finally evolve beyond that to enlightenment.

Chapter 16

Level 2: Enlightenment

The Mind

After awakening, your attention moves to the mind. The mind is a vaster expanse to explore than the body. It is subtler than the body and exceedingly difficult to see. It is not tangible, and hence it is difficult to assess. The mind can almost be defined as the opportunity to clearly see things beyond their appearance because we're now no longer attached to our bodies' limitations.

When you enter the mental realm, it is as if you dissect what is around you. You break everything down into different pieces and learn every element of the object. For example, you meet a new person, and you don't just want to talk to them because you are attracted to them physically, but you want to know more about them. You want to find out where they were born, their interests, what they like doing, what they enjoy, and how their life has been so far. In this way, you engage intellectually. You move from outer to inner, which is the first step of entering from the gross to the subtle.

But learning more and more about everything you see, by breaking every object down and finding out what it is made of and how it is constructed, you begin to explore your mind. This inquiry starts by questioning everything you see by exploring everything you come across.

Once you explore everything in-depth and gain enough knowledge and understanding of it, you'll reach a point of understanding your own mind. You begin questioning yourself, your purpose, your plan, and what you're meant to achieve. You will begin to dissect yourself at this point to look where the truth is hidden inside of you. But you will soon realise that this is not the way to find who you are and eventually learn to come out of this habit.

You realise that the knowledge gained from your young age until now needs to dissolve as you still cannot find here what you were looking for. You realise that truth does not exist in knowledge, and you begin to discard others' opinions. Only after examining and rejecting knowledge from others, including mine, will you be able to see the truth by yourself. You need to find your own truth, and it is not in the mind.

Even though the body exists in the present, the mind exists in the past and future. The mind's character makes it exceedingly difficult to stay in the present; it prefers the past and the future. The mind can travel many directions—many years behind, many years ahead. Hence clarity of mind happens only when it is still.

As you go deeper and deeper into the mind, you learn how to travel as far back as possible; you gather and dissect information and understanding from the past to project the future.

This quality of the mind, which is now trained to travel back and forth, creates confusion. It's as if you forget where you are—you get lost in the past, project into the future, and forget the present. Even though you initially gained the ability to see that what's inside you was fascinating, you are somehow slowly getting lost in your own mind.

We've moved from one attachment to another. The deeper you go into your mind, the stronger the attachment to knowledge. You find that you're not present anymore; you're now lost in the past and the projected future. You will notice you can spend months and even years trying to learn about the very root of the mind itself.

The mind can pierce through any object, breaking it down to absorb its essence. Once the knowledge is absorbed, the object is discarded. This knowledge becomes a memory, which is then used to project the future, allowing us to protect ourselves.

As the mind discovers and absorbs knowledge, confusion and doubt arise. It begins to wonder about its purpose.

For example, during my life, I wore many labels—daughter, friend, student, teacher, wife. Yet, I was none of them. My intellectual essence had no identity. The truth of the mind had no identity, yet it is an image of everything. In reality, it is empty; it has no existence of its own. The mind cannot discover the truth; it can only project the truth. Understanding the right function of the mind and using it for its purposes, such as memory, calculations, thinking, and planning, is the right use of it. It is not the right tool for discovering who we are.

The ability to free the mind from many identifications—from our parents, family, relatives, or any other influence while growing up—allows us to dissolve all falseness. Coming out of the mind is our path to enlightenment. It helps us come out of our old conditionings and limiting beliefs which have always been the cause of our many failures in life. You will realise by penetrating, dissecting, understanding, and observing the different problems, patterns, and identities of the mind, and finally trusting one's heart completely, you can come out of the mind maze.

Enlightenment can be described as an experience where the last identification of who you are in this world falls off. It is the breakaway of all limitations in life, and you are left at the very ground of creation. Creation is the ground of all manifestations, the origin of all things. From here, a new being emerges and expands into a new reality. This reality seems to have no previous conditioning, knowledge, violence, desires, attachments, or identifications of the past; it is the home of peace and home of self.

The process of enlightenment is similar to awakening in the sense that it is a bigger wake-up call showing that you are not just your true self but also a new being. You knock on the door of creation here and see its workings from the very root of it. You observe how reality is formed and experience the higher level of creation here. You see and learn the way manifestation takes place. You see the truth!

You now see the shift in attention takes place again. Most of the attention from the mind is moved to the emotions, and your level of true self is also opened to an extent. Again, we now have four levels of being operating in us simultaneously—the body, mind, emotions, and true self.

During My Process of Enlightenment, I Realised These Truths

As I deepened my spirituality, I felt as though I was shown the start and finish of creation in a nutshell. I felt like it had four phases, as listed below. Intellectually, this may be difficult to follow, but I wanted to share it with you anyway.

Power and Creation

When our limitations of self entirely dissolve, the power within us can reach the ground of creation, giving birth to a new being, born with the essence of truth and intelligence.

Power is seen as curative energy with the nature of clarity and newness. It has a quality of order, purity, creativity, freshness, and rejuvenation.

Creation is experienced as an empty space, seat of manifestation, place of birth, ocean of love, and being at home.

Comprehension of Truth and Intelligence

Truth is the perfect fruit of creation and power. It is realised as the actuality of everything, how things are in their true form, without any distortion or having any prerequisite knowledge.

Intelligence is the ability to observe the manifestation of truth continually.

A Brief Understanding of Reality and New Being

A new being is born from the union of power and creation with the quality of intelligence. This new being grows and expands into a new reality.

Reality employs a continuous movement of power, creation, intelligence, and truth, happening cyclically. Each cycle creates a new reality, continually growing and expanding the new being. Reality promotes oneness which occupies the material of all things.

Consciousness, Bliss, and Existence

Reality appears to grow and expand. When it is amplified, it reaches a point where it becomes aware of itself. When reality is aware of itself, it becomes still. This stillness opens consciousness.

Reality can also be explained as the deflection of consciousness. Consciousness is seen as the source of reality. When reality is still, consciousness enters first, appearing as a mirror. This is the first glance of reality, looking at itself entirely in the mirror of consciousness. Reality sees itself as an objective self through the mirror of consciousness. Living in peace opens consciousness.

When consciousness becomes a reality, you find bliss. Bliss is the ecstasy of experiencing consciousness within you. Consciousness then communicates with the new being to become new consciousness—an advanced human being. This being lives in a state of objective reality.

Consciousness is the essence of existence. It is the original material of all there is. When consciousness expands, you experience existence as the totality of everything.

Level 3: True Love

The Emotions

We attach ourselves to many things we call love. Love is different from attachment. Love offers freeness; attachment offers pain and suffering.

Attachment happens quickly—we don't even realise that we've become attached to things. Attachment occurs when you look at something, and your heart opens towards it. You give yourself completely to the object; it's almost like you don't exist anymore.

For example, if you look at a beautiful house, and immediately your heart opens—this opening of the heart almost allows you to become the house at that moment, freeing yourself. You had lost your sense of identity for a moment, which is exhilarating. Then, your mind wants to possess the house; You heart has opened to. In this way, you become attached to what was beautiful before.

This is the attachment we call love. Love occurred in the beginning when you were admiring the object, but then everything comes tumbling down as attachment sets in to hold on to the object. We experience this attachment with objects first, then move on to the knowledge, then to people, then to oneself, and finally to one's creativity before it is set free.

This attachment cycle deepens quickly and creates emotional baggage. When we are in our twenties, we are emotional. Our love leading to attachments forms with many people around us—we become emotionally connected. In later years, our attachments become larger. In some cases, we attach to people so deeply; sometimes, we even give ourselves up entirely for them. Often, this is what we call love.

We keep saying, "I love you more than anything in the world; I love you more than myself." Quite clearly, we have become a slave to that person. Giving up ourselves, becoming unconscious, and letting that person take control and passively controlling them also is emotional attachment.

It is healthy to admire the thing that we love. However, emotions, love, and compassion need to be clearly and consciously understood to break the bonds of emotional attachment. If you are attached to something, how can you be free? If you're not free, you are bound to feel suffocated; this suffocation causes emotional overwhelm.

Attachment leads us to want to give that person everything and show them how much you care, how much you obey, how much of yourself you give up pleasing them. How can this be called love when you give up everything to please the other, to make the other happy, and make yourself lonely?

Giving oneself up can never be called love; in reality, it is bondage, and bondage causes suffering for both. If this emotional attachment were love in its truest form, why would it be painful when we break up, lose our loved ones, or when loved ones move away?

We have to learn to understand the difference between emotion and love. Emotion arises when we are attached to someone. We unconsciously give ourselves up to someone, and maybe we unconsciously control the other also. It's an unauthorised way of controlling each other. When we learn to love ourselves fully, we love all our goodness and all our faults; this is true love.

When we genuinely love ourselves fully—in every way, not needing someone else's attention to fill that gap—then we know what true love is. True love can only be for ourselves. This true love completes us fully by loving our mind and heart. If our heart looks for somebody else's mind to love when we don't love ourselves fully, it feels incomplete. When our mind looks outside of ourselves to admire somebody else's heart, then this is not wholly loving ourselves.

You are one when mind and heart join together; you cannot tell the difference between mind and heart anymore. When the two have unified, confusion dissolves; they're interlinked, thus balancing each other, providing whole guidance. At this point, they become one. This union is only possible if the mind is free of attachments to knowledge, and the heart is free of attachments to emotions. In this way, true love is the ending of attachments to emotions.

We need to be complete and whole within ourselves first. If you are not complete within yourself, you cannot love someone else; you can only become attached, desiring to fill the gap you feel. When you love yourself completely, then this love overflows to others, and this is shared as true love towards others too. A unified self can love others to complete themselves. An incomplete self cannot help others to feel complete.

When you discover true love within yourself, you now share this true love with everyone around you. This true love now grows and expands to reach many beings. This is a selfless act of oneself and does not expect any recognition or think of gaining anything from others. True love is shown to everyone, and beings who come in contact with such true love can experience healing and have the capacity to recover from many emotional and mental problems.

This true love, when expanded to a greater degree in a genuine form, reveals your true self. The processes of awakening, enlightenment, true love, new consciousness, and liberation affect multiple levels of our being. When you move to another level in your being, you will notice changes in the remaining levels—you will now be functioning from much higher and deeper levels of yourself.

Chapter 18

Level 4: New Consciousness

True Self

Some of us may be lost and searching for something, looking for a deeper meaning to life. We often do not know what we're looking for or how to find it. Even if we stumble across something meaningful, it barely satisfies us. Once again, the search continues after a little or long time of temporary satisfaction.

This search is indeed for reality—the "real" in life. The search is for the true self. We have an aspiration and passion for lasting success, popularity, or happiness. Yet, successful milestones rarely seem to gratify us. This search for success and external gratification may be misunderstood by most of us from a young age.

Once the heart and mind are one and become true love, it then expands to develop into the true self. This reveals who you are at your most essential state. It shows you what you were born as. In my case, even though I grew up observing spirituality and was passionate about it all my life, I never realised that I was a spiritual person. I only saw it in my reflection before, but never as an actuality. I never realised that spirituality represented my true self.

Each of us has a unique true self—yours could be revealed as a musician, writer, sportsman, teacher, carer, or any other path in life. Your true self can also be called your divine self—the state of divinity. You discover your sacred side, the beautiful part of you. All these years of not knowing who you were are now revealed to you openly. It is now the living proof of who you were born as.

This true self is the divine part of you. You could be a musician and enter the divine side of music. You could be running a steel company and develop the divine part of you. It does not mean you have to leave your job or profession and become spiritual in finding your divine self. You only have to learn the way of discovering your true self. It is the next level in you that is looking to open up. The real purpose of your life is revealed there.

This true self is another part of you, other than the body, mind, and emotional experience of yourself that you have come to be. This is the part of you that is here to serve others through this unique gift. This is the gift you were born with, and now is the time for it to be unwrapped.

When you discover your true self, you feel at home. You feel you have been this all your life but were unconscious of it. You have loved this part of you from the very beginning and have only seen this all your life. But somehow, you had ignored it. This is the larger part of you. You feel at ease and feel connected with the now. You feel present in every moment, and everything makes complete sense. Your search comes to an end here. You will learn to express yourself now fully and want to share this divinity with others.

This gift is automatically expressed as nurturing, loving, caring, and giving. There is no other way of describing this. This is your unique quality, and only you can express it this beautifully. It is your way of living life fully and helping others. Nothing will ever confuse you anymore; nothing can distract you anymore as you are fully present. You become the now and continue to expand further.

Once you start to live your divine life by helping and sharing your gift, you grow and develop into a divine being. This true self starts to grow when the old consciousness is completely dissolved. Old conscious, as in, the unconsciousness of us, up until now. The collected parts of ourselves that we were not conscious of while we were still growing up. The unconscious behaviour of the body, mind, and emotions. When all our collection of unconsciousness has been lived and turned into consciousness, our true self grows into its full potential to become new consciousness.

Consciousness means all the seeing in your life from the time of birth until now. To be completely aware of everything happening. When you were born, you did not know who you were, but you try to search and discover it all your life. You are trying to come out of your unconscious life.

From the time you are born to your current age, consciousness is the seer, your knowing. It's the truth. For example, it's only when you are conscious of something you see the truth of it. You can see the tree or eat the fruit from the tree, but only when you are conscious of the tree, it actually exists for you. In the same way, if you are not conscious of something, it does not exist in your life.

This consciousness is the ability to connect and actualize everything with your body. It is the connecting material of all things. Your body can't connect with everything else around it and can only live its own functioning, but consciousness has this ability to connect everything consciously.

The function of the consciousness is the same in its quality but differs only in its content as in the seeing. What I mean by that is, even though we are all born to discover consciousness, our ability to see is different. This is what makes us unique and special individuals. We all have the same functions but experience them differently within us. We all have a body, mind, and emotions, but we use them differently, based on the experiences we desire.

You were born to discover who you are and live this true self completely. Since it has taken years for you to live fully—as you were previously caught up with your mind, body, and emotions—you realize you are only living now when you have discovered your true self.

As soon as you live the life you were born to live consciously, it then expands to become consciousness. In a sense, when the true self lives its actions consciously and is fulfilled, it dissolves in consciousness—then only consciousness exists. Consciousness is fully conscious of itself now. This means you have completed your journey. Consciousness has seen and lived itself fully now, and the journey is complete and ready to give birth to a new consciousness.

Chapter 19

Level 5: Liberation

When you are fully aware of your entire journey from birth to its completion, you are ready to take on a new chapter. When an unconscious life is lived fully, the old consciousness is ready to be dissolved so it can give birth to a completely new consciousness. When this new consciousness enters the body, you become a new individual, a new being. This newly born individual is unique and compassionate. The new consciousness born from the unconsciousness has a powerful individuality; it's very aware of itself in every way. This new being has no previous attachments, beliefs, or wrong thinking. He/she has a new and individual mind. This new being is born with immense compassion for all the other souls who haven't yet discovered who they truly are.

The new being has its own seeing and doing and does not work under the others' control. An enormous amount of energy, power, and will inspires this new being to spread compassion to everyone. This compassion coming from the new being is newness, pure, creative, and transformational.

When this compassion is transmitted to others, their lives begin to transform. They create something new on this planet, intending to expand human consciousness. The new being sees everything as new, each moment, and now lives in this newness constantly. This new being is constantly creative in nature and brings new seeing into this world. This individual bears the responsibility to help others who are stuck in their previous consciousness—old consciousness.

The new being likely had a difficult journey to reach their new consciousness and now wants to help others in their path of self-transformation. Helping others brings tremendous joy and peace. When new beings help other souls discover their true purpose through compassion, their consciousness expands. This expansion of compassion enriches lives and expands the new being to merge with one's breath itself. This combined energy of new beings and their life force rises and extends above the crown area. Consciousness is moved out and resides above one's head until it eventually merges with existence itself. This new being is now merged with all that there is. You can call it universal being, or universal existence.

When a new being is now unified with existence, this process is liberation. As new consciousness becomes one with the breath, it expands and moves out of the body to join the universal being. The sense of individuality, the feeling of I, moves beyond the body and harmonises with existence itself. This freeing of consciousness leads to liberation and internal peace. Nothing inside claims individuality; you become one with all that is. No more separation exists; you're now free from your small, self-trap of being inside your human body. You are one with existence itself. You are one with all that is!

Part 4

Purpose of The School for Enlightenment

Chapter 20

Who is a true seeker?

The true seeker looks below the surface and explores the deepest realms of himself or herself. This person is ready to learn, listen, experiment, and take action. Most importantly, the desire stems from wanting to understand the self better and a wish to help humanity.

The true seeker goes beyond dabbling with spirituality; he/she goes the extra mile and desires to become an advanced spiritual being. Many people are interested in spirituality because it is trendy, or they hear it is something healthy to do. However, the true seeker yearns for self-transformation. He/she wants to develop herself and find their life's purpose. He/she wants to live a life of peace and extend that peace to others.

The quest for meaning is not a passing fancy; it is life's passion. The true seeker lives and breathes spirituality, always moving toward a life of liberation and unity with the Universe.

What is the soul?

The soul is the deepest part of who you are. Without spiritual awakening, we often remain entangled in this world—living a non-soul or partial-soul life. Following a spiritual path frees you to find and live your soul purpose.

You discover your soul by finding your essence, your true self, and from this place, you begin to serve humanity. Through introspection, you explore what inspires you to help others. Acting on this greater purpose contributes to peace and harmony in the world. When you find and act on this charitable and creative nature within you—your soul purpose—you generate an everlasting internal peace and expand that peace to the planet.

As mentioned before, the awakening process begins with detachment from your body. When you're no longer concerned about your physical appearance, you release anxiety-inducing social pressures and learn to accept yourself as you are—embracing the parts of you that near perfection and the parts of you that remain imperfect.

The desire for physical perfection does not fulfil the soul. Instead, the simple act of eating healthfully and exercising in moderation—when we do it for ourselves rather than to please others—is enough. When you reach an awakened state, you begin to use your body lovingly rather than abuse it. You realise that you are not your body; your true essence is far more than your physical form.

Over time you release your identification with external things. You'll begin to understand knowledge in a new way. Similar to the treatment of your body, when you reach an enlightened state, you begin to use your mind lovingly rather than abuse your mind. An awakened mind is another tool, like the body. You use it to live your life—to be the best person you can be, and to be of service to others.

The next step in awakening is creating the union of the enlightened mind and your true tender heart. Your heart and mind admire and love each other and do not obsess over external idols. You no longer emotionally attach to others; you are complete within yourself, catalysing to your true self.

Once you recognise your true self and live your complete life by serving others and fulfilling your passion and purpose, you expand to your full consciousness. Your journey is completed, giving rise to a new consciousness.

This new consciousness enters the body to create a new being who is compassionate and real. At this stage, your living actions are to help others discover their true self and live their true life.

When the new being expands and starts to raise human consciousness, the being starts to merge with the life force to be liberated. You can no longer separate yourself from universal wisdom. The individual has now integrated with everything—the individual consciousness directly connects with the existence.

When everything is in harmony, life feels effortless. In this stage, you are merged with silence, stillness, peace, beauty, and love. They're intertwined, synchronous, and work in multiple dimensions. You flow with everything.

This entire spiritual awakening leads you to discover your soul purpose—you learn what you were born on this earth to do. When you find your true self and expand your consciousness, you realise your soul purpose. By finding your soul, you live a soulful life, and this soulful life exists to serve humanity.

When you have awakened, the gift of the soul comes through. Through this gift, you unleash the wisdom of your soul. Take a moment to reflect and see what you've done over this lifetime. What do you do that you enjoy, which also helps humanity? Check and see if you notice a pattern that underlies your tasks and actions.

For example, you could be a stockbroker. All you've seen growing up is how to make money or how to double your investment on a transaction. You've learned these skills from a young age, and they come naturally to you. As a young trader, you may have been greedy or obsessive. But somehow, you've had an awakening. An unexpected door opened, and you followed a spiritual path. You've reviewed your past habits and detached from the greed; you've refined and polished your skillset now that you're fully conscious.

Your true self recognises that your soul purpose is using your existing skills for the betterment of others. So perhaps now you help other stock traders not only make money but teach them how to do it without greed, obsession, or addiction. You help them find their way out of the shadows to realise their true self and soul purpose. Those people you've helped go on to help others.

Or perhaps you grew up disliking your body. You abused it and made yourself miserable in the process. Yet somehow, the door to spiritual awakening opened for you, and you found your true self, your soul purpose. You learned to love and take care of your body, and you're inspired to help others who struggle with their bodies find peace. Perhaps your soul purpose leads you to become a health professional, gym instructor, or nutritionist. Whatever role you choose, you consciously live your life and help others realise how to live theirs consciously too.

Serving others with the tools that are innate to you is your soul purpose. You're connected to and inspired by divine wisdom, and your actions are pure. You are fulfilled, and you extend an abundance of love into the world.

What is our true identity?

When we were children, we often liked to dress up—maybe as spiderman, superwoman, a cowboy, or princess. We wore these costumes and roles for fun, taking on different personas.

But what we might not recognise is how often we adopted the personas or identities of our parents. Usually, their personality traits are unconsciously embedded within us. Good or bad, they sometimes had a firm hold on us and influence how we live our lives.

For example, if my father liked to play golf and I saw him enjoy the game, then I'd want to play golf also. It might not be a conscious decision; instead, I'm mimicking what I see. Perhaps I play whether I enjoy the game or not.

Or, as another example, if my mother loved wearing beautiful clothes and loved to spend hours in the shops creating just the right outfits, I might also want to wear beautiful clothes. Again, it may not be a conscious decision; I might simply join her on shopping trips, not knowing alternatives were available to me. I may not realise that she was the one who loved shopping for and wearing beautiful clothes and that I was just going along.

We wear these roles unconsciously. When we're young, we use them to shape our identities. We wanted to be like our parents, like superheroes. We did not yet know we could choose for ourselves. We spend a fair amount of time pretending to be something we're not.

We also play roles within our families—daughter, son, mother, father, cousin, brother, sister. Those roles may not have as much meaning as some, but they still come with expectations and responsibilities.

Yet, when we follow a spiritual path and become awakened, our identities become clear.

In my case, when I arrived in England, I had an unfamiliar sense of freedom. I felt I could become whoever I wanted. I had an opportunity to try on many identities to see which felt like the right fit. I wanted to be a hairdresser. I wanted to be a fashion designer. I wanted to be a businesswoman, an accountant, a receptionist, a chef; I had an endless list of roles I wanted to try. Yet, none of the jobs suited me. I tried one after the next, and nothing felt right.

During this time, I noticed one underlying factor. It had been a part of me from my earliest days. I realised that spirituality was woven into my being, and I brought it into all of the roles I tried. Yet, it never occurred to me that perhaps being who I am best suited me, which was to be a spiritual teacher.

Trying on all these roles in England was difficult and tiresome. But without trying so many and eventually resting during a moment of exhaustion, I wouldn't have seen that at the core of everything I tried was an essence of spirituality.

This spiritual person is what I call my true self. It is not an identity or role I wear due to the influence of others. It is the real me. It is the essence of me that I was born with. It will be my core all day, every day until I die. Each of us has a true self, but most of us have not yet uncovered it.

We need to consciously examine how we show up in life—examine the roles we play and the identities we wear. Explore each of the characters you present to others, and see if you can determine which one is indeed yours. This process will eventually help you see your true self.

What is reality?

Once you discover your true self, you begin to live in reality. With reality comes clarity—an absence of false identification with other people, objects, or labels. You begin to see the truth without distortion.

When you discover your true self, you understand more than you ever did before, and this true self is fed by creativity every moment, leaving you to become a new being to move through life in a new way—the true self, reality, and creativity travel hand-in-hand.

Reality exists only for the true self, the pure self. Everything, in reality, is just what it is, without identification of any kind. You attain a deep sense of being at home. When everything is at peace with itself, you find harmony. Once you realise who you are, you learn to love everyone for who they are and let everyone live their individual lives.

Annoyance, dissatisfaction, and sadness arise when you do not yet know who you are. These traits appear when you are displeased with yourself—when you blame others and want to change them.

Once you walk the spiritual path, find your true self and realise your purpose in life, you become entirely you and accept others just as they are. The acceptance of self and others leads to compassion.

What is compassion?

Once you've discovered your true self and connect with your true reality, the experience becomes multidimensional. You know your body, your mind, your heart, and your true purpose.

This new consciousness was born from your unconscious, but at a galactic level. The true self is more in terms of the divine world, whereas new consciousness is in a galactic dimension.

On my spiritual journey, when I embodied my new consciousness, I saw that my consciousness was born out of an immense mass of beautiful stars. I sensed this new consciousness as a separation from my past, from my unconscious movement through life.

This moment of separation from my past unconscious actions and connection with the divine Universe gave birth to my new consciousness. This separation was a confirmation of individuality. This separation was also a realisation of no return! No longer could I return to my petty earthly trappings. I had just begun a new journey, a beautiful journey of new consciousness.

When you realise that a new consciousness is born out of the home of unconsciousness, you will see this new consciousness grow and expand. This growth arises from living in new consciousness every moment of life. Consciousness harmonises with the action of life. We live in awe—with total openness and freeness—waiting to see what happens next.

Living with identifications and attachments was the way of the past, the way of the unconsciousness. This new consciousness does not live with any preconceived ideas, dogmas, or beliefs. It lives every moment with freshness and newness.

This new consciousness has a strong nature of compassion—compassion for unconscious souls. It also has a quality of individuality—individuality of seeing and acting from the true self rather than by the influences of others or the past. It has the virtue of deep seeing and listening to every soul.

The primary purpose of this new consciousness, your new being, is to free others from unconsciousness.

How to harmonise with the Universe?

Through the practise of questioning everything and observing what you see, feel, and think, you can purify your external issues. Through the process of deep meditation, you turn your focus inward and find answers offered by divine universal guidance. Being aware of oneself fully means balancing and integrating the physical experiences of external life with the spiritual and cosmic experiences of inner life.

Once you reach the state of harmonising with the Universe and becoming a new being, your life experiences become subtly different. You discover the unity of the internal and external universe. All aspects of life become intertwined, become one, always moving in a spiral.

As your spiritual connection deepens, you'll realise you're not a limited being—you are the Universe itself. What you experienced during enlightenment manifests universally hereafter.

Consciousness is the connection between a human being and the Universe. This perfect connection is full consciousness—a completed journey. The enlightenment of a new being is also an enlightenment of the Universe. They are synchronised, and communication is established.

This new enlightened being now represents the Universe—the human form of the Universe. Their thoughts, feelings, and actions will manifest not only on earth but also universally. In this way, we create our universe. A conscious creation is a creation of love in the universe. An unconscious creation is a creation of disruption in the universe.

If we can awaken, enlighten, realise our true self, and experience a new consciousness, we will consciously and intentionally create a loving, beautiful, and peaceful universe. If we can liberate ourselves, we can then see the larger reality. We can see that we are a universal being, and what we do matters. We play an essential part in life's unfolding, and our existence is the real truth!

Chapter 21

The School For Enlightenment

The School for Enlightenment's mission is to help guide everyone into an enlightenment experience and teach all people how to find a state of internal peace.

If you have tried to discover who you are, look to find a deeper meaning to life, or struggle with the pressures of the modern world, join us. The school helps you learn simple and effective practises, so you gain more insight into your life. The primary practises are—*Power Flow, Empty Through Living, The Essence of Questioning, Observing the Truth, Mirror of Consciousness, and Freeing of Consciousness.*

The School for Enlightenment helps you discover your true self by assisting you to learn and practise effective techniques useful in your everyday life. These practises help you heal and live your life fully by deconditioning, unloading, and freeing yourself from any desires, attachments, and identifications you may have. Through these practises, you enhance and empower your way of living by gaining pure energy, clarity, and creativity.

The school assists you in the mastery of these practises, so you become enlightened and transform into a new being.

You will learn to differentiate between truth and falsity, reality and fantasy, violence and peace—you'll begin to live a life of authentic contentment.

The School for Enlightenment website shares true stories of my spiritual journey. I explain how I developed the practises I teach—the practises I share briefly in this book. By learning how to embody your new being, you'll deepen your compassion, peace, love, and harmony with the world. This compassion and altruism is the future language of the world. You'll learn a new method of communicating with the divine Universe and other human beings. Ignorance and judgement will fall to the side.

By bringing this new way of thinking and being into this world, the School for Enlightenment helps everyone find their true self and experience a new consciousness. This book shared with you my struggle to find an accessible spiritual teacher, and I want to make your journey easier.

Through The School for Enlightenment, I am here for you. I wish you immense peace and love in your heart and a beautiful new reality.

What Is the Source of the School's Intention?

We all have intentions in life which may include educating people, spreading the word of peace, attempting to save the world, getting rid of poverty, providing better health to others, and so on. Intentions are often beautiful. They are thoughts turned into actions.

But every intention is supported by a source. Is the source of my intention just a good intention? Or is the source of my intentions borne from a need for greed? What is the source of my intentions? Are my intentions driven by my body, my feelings, my mind, or something else?

Due to my spiritual journey, the source of my intention is a new consciousness. A consciousness that has not been here before—a new consciousness is pure with no knowledge of the past and no propagation of the future.

Connection to the source that arises from new consciousness automatically leads to true action. The School for Enlightenment was born from my connection with the universal source—it embraces the teachings and intentions of love and peace.

Who Should Attend The School For Enlightenment?

If you're looking to advance and develop in your life, if you're looking for a spiritual direction, The School for Enlightenment is for you.

It is for those who struggle in everyday life and are looking for advice; it's for those with emotional problems or heightened stress. The school is for everyone, but it's best suited for true spiritual seekers keen to discover the truth of life. Most of all, it is for those who want to go to the very depth of the mind and soul and discover the meaning of existence itself.

Your learning process is tailored to your needs. The different practises are discussed in understandable terms, and I'll help you determine which practise to start with. You will waste no time learning something that may not be useful or too advanced.

The length of your spiritual journey depends on you. The journey to the new being and liberation is different for everyone. However, trust that you'll be supported on the path no matter where you begin or how long it takes. Your experience depends on your level of commitment and passion for discovering your true self.

Who Do I Contact for Spiritual Support?

The School for Enlightenment wants to make access to spiritual instruction simple and easy. In the twenty-first century, online learning is accessible to nearly everyone. Visit the website www.theschoolforenlightenment.com, and you'll find various methods for contacting us—phone, email, or contact form.

Once I receive your message, I'll contact you and go through the initial process of discovering where you are in your journey so I can tailor your lessons for you.

If you need spiritual support with any of the following, I am here to assist you in your spiritual journey.

- Discovering your true self
- Finding or defining your spiritual goals
- Discovering suitable spiritual practises for your personal development
- How to live a spiritual life without affecting your day-to-day life
- Clarifying spiritual misconceptions that hinder your path to self-discovery
- Help with recovering your passion for spiritual growth and gain deeper insights

- Clearing doubts and confusions to help you progress quickly on your journey to enlightenment
- Assisting you in gaining clarity and intelligence on your way to self-transformation and becoming a new being

Get in Touch

- info@theschoolforenlightenment.com

Chapter 22

The Programs

The School for Enlightenment offers five spiritual programs.

Level 1: Awaken Your Inner Power Program

In this program, you will learn to understand how to harness the power within you through simple practises. You will learn techniques that will offer you clarity, calmness, and expanded energy. You will reduce your stress, gain the capacity to see the world differently, and enhance your life's success. You will gain the power to transform your life in a beautiful way. With simple daily practises, you will be able to see the changes and benefits in a couple of weeks. When continued for a long time, it will lead to your awakening.

Level 2: Mind Mastery Signature Program

In this program, you will learn to discover your mind's real nature by exploring the deeper layers and extracting the intricate connections between thinking, knowledge, and identifications of your mind. This program is an easy way to learn all the complicated functions of the mind and master the solutions to its common problems. Through various methods and practises, you will be able to overcome your mental problems and use your mind as a tool. After applying these methods over a long period of time, it will lead to enlightenment.

Level 3: Self Discovery Premium Program

In this program, you will acquire an in-depth understanding of the self. We will also focus on many hidden layers of the self and its activities in detail. You will gain clarity by learning the different functions of the self so you can detach from its negative attachments and use it in the right way, which leads to discovering who you are. By using various techniques and practises, you can discover your life's purpose and what you were born to do. When you continue to apply these practises, you will discover your true self, which then leads to actualising your purpose.

Level 4: Creating a New Consciousness Program— Pre-Qualification Required

In this program, we will discover that consciousness is the source of all-seeing. This is an advanced practise, which facilitates opening to a new consciousness. In this practise, you will learn to recognise your old consciousness and learn the ability to harness the newness—experiencing bliss. This leads to a state of individuality and develops compassion. Continued practise leads to a higher state of being and the most powerful state to create a new life.

Level 5: The Program for Supreme Freedom—
Pre-Qualification Required

In this program, you will learn to overcome the ever-present "I" with you. This constant feeling of "I" has been with us for a long time. It has been the foundation of all our life's activities. Through this method, you will learn to become liberated, leading to the union with existence itself. This practise is advanced, and a sustained, continued approach to this method will free your consciousness and lead to internal peace.

Please note that while I, Smitha Jagadish, have extensive experience as a spiritual teacher, I am not a psychologist, psychotherapist, physician, or other licensed health care professional.

This book is based on my own life experiences and methodology. The information provided in this book is educational and is presented only as general information; it is not medical or psychological advice.

Any advice presented in this book regarding the practises taught at The School for Enlightenment is not intended to diagnose, cure, treat, or prevent any medical problem or psychological disorder. In addition, this advice is not a substitute for seeking professional health care advice and services.

I advise you to seek professional advice as appropriate before making any decisions regarding your current state of physical and mental health.

Acknowledgements

I want to express my gratitude to my parents for giving birth to me and raising me, as I was not an easy child. I immensely appreciate all the love, knowledge, and values they gave me and that they taught me to work toward becoming a better human being right from the start.

I want to express my love to my dearest brother, who has been with me throughout my life's ups and downs. I thank him immensely for all his support throughout my journey.

I want to thank my closest and dearest friend, who knows me more deeply than anyone else, and suggested I write this book to help and free other souls like me!

My special thanks go to my husband and my children, who I love very dearly and have been my rock throughout my life. Without their understanding, this journey would not have been impossible.

Author Bio

Smitha Jagadish has had a love for spirituality since she was a little girl. She always keenly observed life and enjoyed expressing herself through writing. During her spiritual quest, she realised she was born spiritual and lived an authentic spiritual life to the fullest. She often jokes, "Even though I am married with children, I have been living a spiritual life of a guru within."

Smitha writes because she loves to share her insights and creativity with the world, inspiring freedom and a way forward to transforming lives, one soul at a time.

Smitha resides in beautiful England with her husband and children. She writes nonfiction books about awakening, enlightenment, life purpose, transformational practises, and inner peace. She also runs an online spiritual school helping many students to clarify spiritual doubts, and guides several spiritual seekers to enlightenment through her coaching programs. She wishes to encourage and help everyone to live a life of peace.

www.ingramcontent.com/pod-product-compliance
Lightning Source LLC
Chambersburg PA
CBHW031340060726
47590CB00007B/2561